SCOTT JOPLIN
Collected Piano Works

SCOTT JOPLIN

1868-1917

SCOTT JOPLIN
Collected Piano Works

EDITED BY VERA BRODSKY LAWRENCE

Editorial Consultant Richard Jackson

Introduction by Rudi Blesh

THE NEW YORK PUBLIC LIBRARY

This edition distributed by *BELWIN-MILLS PUBLISHING CORP.*

The clothbound edition of THE COLLECTED WORKS OF SCOTT JOPLIN

Volume I *Works for Piano*
Volume II *Works for Voice*

Published by The New York Public Library in 1971

Second Printing July 1972
Third Printing November 1972

The research and preparation for publication of this edition was made possible by a grant from The Rockefeller Foundation.

The edition was designed and prepared under the supervision of Vera Brodsky Lawrence.

Contents

ORIGINAL WORKS

Original Works, continued

COLLABORATIVE WORKS

MISCELLANEOUS WORKS

APPENDIXES

Illustrations, following page xl: Alternate Covers

Editor's Note

THE WORKS OF Scott Joplin published between 1895 and 1917 include fifty-three pieces for piano, ten songs, the opera *Treemonisha,* and three subsequently published, revised excerpts from *Treemonisha.* In all, twenty-one publishers (among them Joplin himself) are known to have brought out his music during his lifetime. Still others published reprints and instrumental arrangements of his compositions.

Joplin's published piano works comprise forty-four original pieces: rags, marches, waltzes, a tango; seven works written in collaboration with other composers; an arrangement of a rag by Joseph F. Lamb: *Sensation;* and the *School of Ragtime—6 Exercises for Piano.* Eight of the ten songs were original compositions—two being later vocal versions of the piano rags *Maple Leaf* and *Pine Apple* [sic]—another the original 1902 version of *The Ragtime Dance* for singer, piano and dancers, of which a shortened arrangement for piano was published in 1906. One of the remaining two songs *Sarah Dear* is Joplin's version of a tune that had been heard in many guises and places from early times on (**page xxix**); the other is an arrangement by Joplin of *Snoring Sampson,* a ragtime song by Harry La Mertha (of which no copy has been found).

Joplin also is known to have arranged a number of his own and other composers' rags for dance orchestra (he most certainly arranged for other instrumental combinations as well). Since published dance orchestra arrangements (at that time often printed in sets of instrumental parts only, without full score or piano-conductor part) did not always identify the arrangers, it is difficult to assess just how many of his works were arranged by Joplin. Whoever the arrangers were, it is a fact, nevertheless, that a great many of his popular rags and marches were arranged and published in various instrumental versions, and that they were widely performed and danced to. The covers of two

piano pieces in this collection advertise their availability in other instrumentations: *The Sycamore* (I:97)†, "Published for Band, Orchestra, Mandolin, Guitar, etc." and *Eugenia* (I:139), "Published for Band and Orchestra." A choice of instrumental accompaniments, complete with prices, is announced on the cover of the song *I Am Thinking of My Pickanniny Days* [sic] (II:285): "Song .50, Orchestration .50, Brass Band .75, Guitar Song .40." No instrumental arrangements are included in this edition.

With editions of nineteen publishers reproduced in these volumes (the omission of the remaining two will be explained later in this note), a colorful variety of music typefaces and printing styles is offered. Together with the evocative cover designs, they present a vivid panorama of the Ragtime Era, contributing a flavor as distinctive, in graphic terms, as the music itself.

Among these cover designs, however, will be found some examples of the offensive stereotyped caricatures of Negroes that were in common use on American sheet music covers from early minstrel-show days until well into the nineteen-thirties. They too were a part of the Ragtime Era, as were the degrading terms and spurious "darkey" sentiments that are found in some of Joplin's song texts. Objectionable as we find them today, they are included since they are indispensable to the historical accuracy of this edition.

The names of Joplin's publishers are mostly unknown to us—indeed many must have been obscure even in their own time. A number of them belonged to the special breed of small music publisher that flourished around the turn of the cen-

---

†Roman and arabic numerals separated by a colon, in parentheses, refer to volume and page numbers in this edition, e.g., (I:97) means Volume I, page 97. NOTE: References to Volume II—or II—apply to the hardcover edition of THE COLLECTED WORKS OF SCOTT JOPLIN, Volume II: Works for Voice, published by The New York Public Library.

tury in out-of-the-way places. They served a significant purpose, providing through their publications the unique means (in pre-sound-recording days) for preserving a large part of our vernacular music.

Each of his publishers, whether obscure or known, contributed his share to the eloquent portrait of Joplin that is found in the collected pages of his published music. To study these pages as a totality provides the documentary means not only for following the creative development of a distinctive artist, but also for evaluating the extent of his contribution to American music.

However, study of the publications also disclosed that their musical, historical, and graphic riches in most cases were flawed by editorial carelessness. Great numbers of errata of various kinds were found throughout. Since this edition is primarily intended for study and performance, it was judged more important that correct (as far as possible) music texts be presented rather than to perpetuate original errors for antiquarian interest. For this reason corrections have been incorporated into the facsimile pages. No changes in musical content have been made. The corrections deal principally with the following categories of errata: incorrect or missing notes, accidentals, harmonies, rhythmic notation, rests, clefs, time signatures, key signatures, key changes, repeat signs, double bars, stems, ties, slurs, augmentation dots, brackets, etc.: also misprints and misspellings in vocal texts. Where the composer's intention was clear—and technical or space limitations inhibited corrections —the following varieties of errata were left unchanged: redundant accidentals; incorrect directions of stems, beams, slurs, ties, etc.; incorrect positions (usually on the wrong side of the right note) of accents, *staccatos, marcatos, fermatas,* etc.

Joplin's *Treemonisha* revisions (shown in his own hand in the two-page illustration following the Preface in Volume II) have been incorporated into the score (II:170-171) as well as the types of corrections listed above. One addition has been made: the missing but logical tempo indication at the beginning of *The Corn Huskers* (II:36),

[Allegretto $\unicode{x2669} = 84$] has been supplied in square brackets. This metronome indication is derived from the 2/4 Allegretto occurring at the bottom of the same page, an obvious resumption of tempo after the intervening bars of Largo in 4/4.

All fingerings, pedals, and dynamics are presumably Joplin's. Two characteristic dynamic indications are found throughout the piano pieces, *f-p* and *p-f: f-p* means that the section is to be played *forte* the first time and *piano* the second; *p-f* of course indicates the reverse.

Where the musical intention is clear, typographical eccentricities peculiar to certain music setting techniques have been retained for their visual charm and flavor. For examples, see *Cleopha* (I:47) and *The Favorite* (I:93), with their odd treatments of double barlines and repeat signs (obviously proper symbols were not available to the typographers). Other quaint music symbols are found in these pieces, in *The Sycamore* (I:97), and in other publications in this collection.

The copy of *Cleopha* presents a puzzling inconsistency as well: the plate identifications at the bottoms of the second, third, and fourth pages (I:49-50-51) give, surprisingly, the title *The Conductor*. Whether this was an editor's or printer's error, or if it represents a last-minute decision to change the title from *The Conductor* to *Cleopha* will probably remain an unsolved mystery. Also mysterious, but perhaps less so, is the blurb appearing on the first page of music of *The Ragtime Dance* (1902 version) (II:291) which lists, among other Joplin titles, *A Gentle Breeze*. Since there is no known Joplin composition of that name, it seems most probable that *A Gentle Breeze* evolved into the more commercial-sounding *A Breeze from Alabama* (I:53), also published in 1902.

Among uncorrected non-musical errata, a number of misspellings, occurring chiefly on covers, will be found. The word "pickaninny" is misspelled in the cover title of the song, viz, *I Am Thinking of My Pickanniny Days* (II:285); the caption title gives the correct spelling. A recurrent misspelling is "Swipsey" for "Swipesy," appearing in blurbs listing Joplin "hits" on three covers: *Peacherine* (alternate cover, seen in the section of alternate covers following the Introduction in Volume I), *Lily Queen* (I:257) and *A Breeze from Alabama* (I:53), which also informs that the work is "Dedecated [sic] to P. G. Lowery, World's Challenging Colored Cornetist and Band Master." "Swipsey" is also seen in the copy of *"Swipesy—Cake Walk* itself (I:239), in the plate identification at the bottom of the second page of music. *Augustan Club* appears as "Augustain Club" in a blurb on the cover of *Sunflower Slow Drag* (I:245) which slightly metamorphoses, in its own caption title, to *Sun Flower Slow Drag.* Following the caption title *The Crush Collision March,* the cover title of which is *Great Crush Collision—March* (I:3), Joplin is credited as the "Author of the Combintion March" [sic].

Inconsistencies between cover and caption titles and subtitles abound. Some examples: the cover title *A Breeze from Alabama—A Ragtime Two Step* (I:53) is followed by the caption title *A Breeze from Alabama—March and Two Step;* the cover information *Rosebud—Two Step* (I:121) is followed by the caption information *The Rose-Bud March; Nonpareil (None to Equal)* (I:163) on the cover becomes *The Nonpareil—A Rag & Two Step* in the caption; *Something Doing—Cake Walk March* (I:251) becomes *Something Doing— A Ragtime Two Step.*

Apart from the editorial casualness it reflects, this substitution of terms would also indicate that the designations: cakewalk, march, two-step, rag, and slow drag were interchangeable, inasmuch as they alluded to a genre of music in duple meter to which a variety of dance steps might be performed.

Some of these inconsistencies might have been dictated by the esthetic considerations or space requirements of cover designers, e.g., the cover title *The Chrysanthemum—An Afro-Intermezzo* (I:107) changes its subtitle in the caption to the lengthier *An Afro-American Intermezzo* (which in 1904 may have been one of the earliest applications of the term to a published musical work).

The inconsistently used terms, "ragtime," "rag time," and "rag-time"; also "two-step," "two step,"

and "twostep" are treated in each case as originally printed, in both the Contents and Index. All titles in the Contents refer to cover titles and subtitles; both cover and caption information are supplied in the Index.

Some discrepancies exist between the dates of printed copyright notices and the actual dates of copyright registration. Thus, *I Am Thinking of My Pickanniny Days* (II:285), *Maple Leaf Rag— Song* (II:309), and *Eugenia* (I:139), respectively bearing printed copyright notices dated 1901, 1903, and 1905, were registered in 1902, 1904, and 1906, respectively.

Works showing printed copyright notices, but for which no actual copyrights were registered are: *March Majestic* (I:71) and *The Strenuous Life* (I:77), both dated 1902; *Rosebud—Two-Step* (I:121), dated 1905, *Nonpareil (None to Equal)* (I:163), dated 1907, and *Pine Apple Rag—Song* (II:325), dated 1910. *Leola—Two Step* (I:125), dated 1905, oddly enough, bears an English copyright, the printed copyright notice reading, "Entered at Stationer's Hall, London."

The 1911 copyright notice appearing on the revised excerpt from *Treemonisha, Prelude to Act 3* (II:255) was obviously an error or an oversight. According to the Copyright Office report it was registered ". . . following publication Dec. 15, 1913." The report adds, "Copyright is claimed on alterations and additions of a few notes." For editorial consistency the Contents lists the work in its correct chronological sequence, following the *Treemonisha* excerpt *A Real Slow Drag* (II:237), copyrighted July 15 1913. The date in parentheses (1911) refers to the printed copyright notice, as do all dates listed in the Contents. Detailed original copyright information is given in the Index.

Where more than one cover design for a given work was found, it was not always clear which had been the first edition. Copies seen at The Library of Congress that had been stamped for copyright registration unquestionably were first editions, but sheet music obtained from private sources sometimes presented puzzling decisions. The problem was made more complex by the publishers' practice of frequently changing cover designs when issuing reprintings (without dates) while the music pages—usually reprinted from the original plates—remained unchanged. In doubtful instances where no clues could be found in the printed copies, scholars and collectors were consulted. To the best of our knowledge, the covers chosen for these volumes are first editions. Any substantiated information to the contrary would be welcomed by the editor.

The acknowledgment to "The American Tobacco Co., Manufacturers of Old Virginia Cheroots," for permission to use their copyrighted design as cover art for the first edition of *Maple Leaf Rag* (I:25) furnishes an interesting insight into John Stark's financially cautious first steps as a music publisher. Whether a permission fee was paid is not known. The elegantly engraved edition with its distinctive cover is a highly prized collector's item today.

Two later covers for *Maple Leaf Rag* appear after the Introduction in Volume I: an early St. Louis edition (probably the second edition) with a maple leaf, Joplin's picture, and a dedication to the Maple Leaf Club; and one of a later edition, omitting the picture and dedication, and bearing the imprint (with a stork) adopted by Stark when he moved to New York in 1905. The alternate cover for *Swipesy—Cake Walk* is one of two alternates that were seen; they do not vary greatly. The one included here is the later edition of the two, showing Stark's New York imprint, testimony that the work enjoyed a long popularity: it was first published in 1900. Also included in this section are alternate covers for *Peacherine Rag* and *The Cascades*.

A great number of the covers were originally printed in color, the colors often having been changed in different printings. In this edition all covers are printed in black and white. It is noted that the cover for *Stoptime Rag* (I:215) has been trimmed across the top. All examples of this cover that were seen had been similarly cropped.

All full-page advertisements, musical and verbal, that had appeared in the original sheet music have been omitted. Included, however, are several small ads, appearing in the bottom margins of three Seminary Music Company publications: *Country Club* (I:197), *Euphonic Sounds* (I:203), and *Pine Apple Rag—Song* (II:325). Because of space limitations it was necessary to delete from the outer margins of *Palm Leaf Rag* (I:89) the pictorial announcement of the then approaching Lewis and Clark Centennial, to be celebrated in Portland, Oregon in 1905.

Although not an original Joplin composition, *Sensation—A Rag* (I:287) by Joseph F. Lamb, arranged by Joplin, has been included among the miscellaneous piano works. The interesting details of how the work came to be published and Joplin's connection with it, as well as information concerning his other composing collaborations, will be found in the following Introduction by Mr Blesh.

Also included among the miscellaneous piano works is *Silver Swan Rag* (I:291) in what may be its first published version. The work, recorded on a player-piano roll, was discovered in 1970 by Albert Huerta, a Los Angles piano roll collector, among a pile of long-since-purchased and forgotten piano rolls stored in his garage. Realizing that it was credited to Joplin, Mr Huerta brought *Silver Swan Rag* to the attention of Richard Zimmerman and other members of the local ragtime society The Maple Leaf Club, who decided to circulate a tape recording of the roll among Joplin scholars for their judgment on its authenticity. It was generally agreed that it was indeed a Joplin composition, although no manuscript nor published copy has ever been known to exist; nor has any reference to the work been found except in 1915-16 catalogs of the QRS Music Company. Mr Huerta's roll had been issued by the National Music Roll Company of St Johnsville, New York. Oddly enough, since his discovery a copy of the QRS roll is reported to have been found. Both rolls are believed to have been released at about the same time (1914-15). Whether they are duplicate versions is not known.

The work as published in this edition was transcribed from the National roll by Donna McCluer and Richard Zimmerman, and subsequently revised and edited by William Bolcom and the editor. Both notation and dynamics are a distillation into idiomatic Joplinesque terms of the music which, as heard on the roll, is encumbered with exaggerations often heard on player-piano rolls of the period.

Since no written or printed copy has so far been found, nor any copyright information or other documentation brought to light, no claim is made here that the work is authentic. *Silver Swan Rag* has been included because of its undoubted interest as a composition attributed to Joplin.

Certain omissions are regretfully noted. An exhaustive search for the long missing score of the unpublished (although copyrighted) ragtime opera *A Guest of Honor* was unsuccessful. In spite of persistent, varied, and recurrent rumors concerning its whereabouts, no factual information has been uncovered to suggest that the score is any longer in existence. As previously stated, no copy has been found of Joplin's arrangement of Harry La Mertha's song *Snoring Sampson,* nor have Joplin's directions for the dance steps to *The Ragtime Dance—Song* (II:291), announced in the sheet music, been located. And, finally, although original editions of all Joplin's piano pieces had been compiled and prepared for this collection, complete publication was prevented by the refusal of Mr Jerry Vogel, the present copyright holder of three works, to grant a permission to include them. As a consequence, *Fig Leaf Rag, Rose Leaf Rag,* and *Searchlight Rag* do not appear in this edition. It is hoped that these fine works will eventually find their rightful places in future editions of Joplin's music.

The above omissions explain the absence in these volumes of two of Joplin's original publishers. A list of all the publishers and their locations will be found following the Index.

Each volume is organized in three sections: Volume I, Works for Piano: Original Works, Collaborative Works, Miscellaneous Works; Volume II, Works for Voice: *Treemonisha—Opera in Three Acts,* Revised Excerpts from *Treemonisha†,* Songs. The works comprising each section are arranged in chronological sequence, according to dates of copyright. In the Contents the titles refer to cover titles and subtitles; the dates in parentheses refer to printed copyright notices. Each volume is individually paginated. The page numbers in the special Table of Contents for *Treemonisha* (II:8), reprinted from the original edition, have been altered to agree with the pagination of Volume II. The Index, appearing in each volume, lists all works in both volumes, giving both cover and caption titles and subtitles, complete original copyright information, original publishers, and other pertinent information. Works that have been omitted from this edition are listed, with asterisks, in the Index for the purpose of supplying complete bibliographical information.

ACKNOWLEDGMENTS

Sincere gratitude is expressed to the many people whose extraordinary cooperation so greatly contributed to the realization of this project. A great part of the rare music reproduced in these volumes was lent by private collectors who in turn enlisted the participation of other private collectors. Not only did they generously provide their sheet music, but also information, advice, help, and encouragement in solving the many complications met during the preparation of this edition.

For the above reasons and many more besides, grateful acknowledgment is given to the following members and honorary members of the ragtime community: Elliot L. Adams, T. J. Anderson, Eubie and Marion Blake, David E. Bourne, Robert A. Bradford, Arnold Caplin, Peter Clute, Roger Hankins, David A. Jasen, Robert E. Kimball, John Maddox, Michael Montgomery, Max Morath, John V. Phelan Jr, Teresa Sterne, Trebor Jay Tichenor, and Guy Waterman. And to

† The second excerpt *Prelude to Act 3,* although not a work for voice, is included in Volume II with the other *Treemonisha* excerpts.

the non-ragtimers: William Lichtenwanger and the Music Division of The Library of Congress, Kurtz Myers and the Grosvenor Reference Division of the Buffalo and Erie County Public Library, and Mrs Bernard A. Smith and the Crouch Library of Baylor University Library.

Special thanks are offered to Rudi Blesh for putting at our disposal rare materials from his collection, among them Joplin's own score of *Treemonisha* with its revisions in his own hand; to William Bolcom for his invaluable assistance in lending an "extra pair of eyes" to the music proofreading and his help with the revisions of *Silver Swan Rag;* to the National Sheet Music Society for publishing in their Newsletter a list of materials being sought; to Addison W. Reed for sharing his newly-found information about the Joplin family; to William Russell, not only for furnishing

otherwise unobtainable sheet music, but also for his learned information concerning ragtime instrumentations of the period; to Richard Zimmerman and the Maple Leaf Club for their interest and help in locating materials, and their cooperation, with Donna McCluer and Albert Huerta, in making *Silver Swan Rag* available.

For cooperation and technical assistance of various kinds, additional special thanks are due to Richard B. Allen of the Archive of New Orleans Jazz of the Howard-Tilton Memorial Library of Tulane University Library, Arthur La Brew, John I. Davis, Alvin Deutsch, William J. Greene, Anthony Landini, Fred Little, Henry K. Rosborne, and Chester Smith.

VBL

Scott Joplin: Black-American Classicist

BY RUDI BLESH

SCOTT JOPLIN, master composer of classic ragtime, was also, for far too long, a classic example of forgotten genius. He was the central figure and prime creative spirit of ragtime, a composer from whom a large segment of twentieth-century American music derived its shape and spirit. Beyond America the European music world felt the captivating force of ragtime's rhythm and the lilt and charm of its melody. Brahms had envisioned a ragtime project just before his death;[1] Debussy experimented in the medium with two piano pieces, *Golliwogg's Cakewalk* and *General Lavine;* Stravinsky followed not too long after with his *Piano Rag Music*. Through it all, Scott Joplin and his seminal creations remained in the background.

A black, one-time itinerant pianist, Joplin led the vanguard of American popular music in the early part of the twentieth century, effecting a basic and altogether remarkable fusion of Afro-American rhythm, American folk song both black and white, and the musical principles and procedures that America has traditionally derived from, and shared with, Europe. A quiet and serious man, Scott Joplin was a forceful and potent musical innovator.

At the turn of the century ragtime was all the rage. America cakewalked to it. So did the French, though they called it *le temps du chiffon*. In Vienna the Prater carousel riders whirled to it and the coffee house zithers played it; the London barrel organs bleated it out; Scotch lassies did their Highland fling while the pipers skirled out the *Maple Leaf Rag*. John Philip Sousa and his concert band carried it to the 1900 Paris Exposition, then were summoned to give command performances for Edward VII, Wilhelm II, and Nicholas II.

As for serious acceptance, ragtime fared better in Europe than at home where its very name was an epithet, a scornful, belittling term with strong racial overtones. Conscious of this, Joplin himself called the appellation "scurrilous." America both accepted and rejected ragtime. Initially, emerging from the red-light districts it became a popular hit of unprecedented proportions. Quickly, then, it began to meet with fanatic opposition from an informal entente of the moralistic prudes, the Europe-oriented culture snobs, and an Academy that felt suddenly challenged. The challenge came from an unexpected source, the people and the open-minded members of the musical establishment (and there were some) who espoused the new music. The real trouble with ragtime was not that it was no good but that it was too good, and it had, so to speak, been born out of wedlock, with at least a part of its parentage black.

A bitter controversy ensued. It filled the air—all but drowning out the music—from 1897 to 1917. Meanwhile a handful of creative spirits, some black, some white—James Scott, Joseph F. Lamb and a few others, led by Scott Joplin—went on composing serious ragtime; getting it published where and when they could, but composing it nonetheless. Finally the decisive factor, commercialization, entered. Tin-Pan Alley, reaching for the quick buck, flooded the market with an inundation of ragtime: mostly spurious, second- and third-rate, occasionally worthy. The public was beginning to tire of it all when a new "illegitimate," ragtime's Storyville child "jass," seized the stage just before we entered World War I. On the very day we entered the war, Scott Joplin died.

Now in 1971, half a century after that event and three-quarters of a century after Scott Joplin composed his keystone piano work, the *Maple Leaf Rag*, we are at last ready to accept this long-rejected American music and to accord it the position it merits. Now an American musicologist can

1 Robert Haven Schauffler *The Unknown Brahms* (New York: Dodd, Mead and Co 1933) 176.

write of Joplin's rags that they "are the precise American equivalent, in terms of a native style of dance music, of minuets by Mozart, mazurkas by Chopin or waltzes by Brahms."[2] In accordance with this new recognition, Joplin's music is being enthusiastically embraced by a new generation of performers and listeners. And, notably, his collected *oeuvre* is receiving publication by one of our great cultural institutions.

With this edition, an all-but-forgotten black-American genius is being honored. This is one point of view. From a broader point of view, a country once honored by Scott Joplin's life and music, is being honored again.

BEGINNINGS

Scott Joplin was born on Tuesday, November 24, 1868 in Texarkana, Texas, the small twin-city divided between two states. His parents were Giles Joplin, a laborer, of North Carolina origin, and Florence Givens Joplin from Kentucky. The mother had been free from birth; the father was an ex-slave, slavery having been legally terminated only five years before Scott Joplin's birth. The Joplins led an intensely musical home life: Giles Joplin played the violin (he had performed as a dance musician during his slavery days) and his wife sang and played the banjo. Scott had an older brother Monroe, and two younger ones: Will, who sang and played the guitar, and Robert, who sang and also composed. Little is known about the musical accomplishments of his two sisters Myrtle and Ossie (or of Monroe) but it may be assumed that they too contributed to the family musical scene.[3]

While very young, Scott played the guitar and, somewhere along the line, blew the bugle. When barely seven he discovered a piano in a neigh-bor's house, and was found surreptitiously experimenting with it. Given an opportunity to express himself, he displayed his natural musical gifts almost immediately. Soon the neighborhood was listening and talking. Giles Joplin, though determined that his son learn a trade, scraped money together and bought a second-hand square piano.

The boy was at this instrument day and night and before he was eleven years old he was improvising so remarkably that he became the talk of the Negro community. Rumors spread to the white community through servants' talk—Mrs Joplin was a laundress.

In those days almost every Midwestern town had its German music teacher, a paragon immersed in the three B's, who generally taught piano and frequently other instruments as well. There was such a man in Texarkana; he heard young Joplin play and as a result gave him free lessons in piano, sight reading, and the principles to extend and confirm his natural instinct for harmony. The professor is said to have played the classics for him and to have talked of the great composers and, especially, of the famous operas.

Many years later, Scott Joplin's widow (who had been his second wife) was able to confirm the story of these events. And, though she could not recall the name of the German teacher, she related that Joplin never forgot his first benefactor. In his later years (1907 to 1917), Mrs Joplin said, he sent his teacher, by then ill and poor, gifts of money from time to time. According to Fred Joplin (Monroe's son), Scott Joplin returned briefly to Texarkana in 1907; and one may assume that he visited his first teacher then. Mrs Joplin also said that when his mother died, just as he was entering adolescence, there was friction with his father over learning a trade, which resulted in his leaving home (he would be followed a little later by Will and Robert). His own departure was about 1882 when he was about fourteen.[4]

2 H. Wiley Hitchcock *Stereo Review* (April 1971) 84.

3 In July 1971, Joplin scholar Mr Addison W. Reed located and interviewed two Joplin nieces in Texarkana, and a nephew in Marshall. The resulting data was kindly made available for this Preface.

4 Mrs Lottie Stokes Joplin, in interviews with Rudi Blesh and Harriet Janis, 1949-50.

THE SPORTING WORLD & THE NEW MUSIC

The move plunged him into the remarkable sub-world of the American honky-tonk and red-light districts where pianists, black and white, were in great demand—this, of course, being in the very infancy of mechanical and recorded music, and long before the era of radio and television. A large, loosely-knit clan of itinerant musicians roamed from town to town, assured of employment anywhere. Wages were nominal: tips ranged from good to famous to princely, depending upon whether the bordello guests were mere visiting cowboys or sports of Diamond Jim Brady status.

At fourteen, Scott Joplin was by no means the youngest piano "professor"—some were known to be as young as twelve. The black lad from Texarkana shuttled from Texas to Louisiana and all over the Mississippi Valley states—Missouri, Arkansas, and Kansas—the region that was the cradle of ragtime. He was now in a different school: adult education for a child. He met hundreds of mainly self-taught musicians and singers, and heard popular music, light classical music, and folk music, old and new, black and white, respectable and not-so-respectable. It would be a prime source of melodic inspiration for the rest of his life.

This was a lurid but vital orbit. It was a partly sub rosa circuit of saloons and bawdy houses, pool halls and all-night cafés, medicine shows and vaudeville (then called "variety"), and the notorious Forty-Niner Camps: nomadic tent shows depicting the dance halls of the California Gold Rush complete with cancan girls authentically *sans culottes* and the larcenous roulette wheel.

It was a hurrying, exciting world of music, wine, and contraband love, a terrain not cosmopolitan but still frontier. Its real music was not Strauss nor Waldteufel nor, even, our own Gottschalk. Nor was it the lugubrious teary ballads of the New York Rialto. It was a heady new music called ragtime, a dance-song alembicated from the native air, an intoxicant bubbling with the spirit of a wholly American time and place.

For a young man marked out to become the greatest composer of this new music, this folk-conservatory was far more valuable than a real conservatory could have been at that moment. It was a world where for the very first time in America black and white musicians were meeting as equals, competing, trading, and borrowing from the musical traditions of their two different races. The music coming out of this meeting was first called "jig piano." (Though "jig" later became a derogatory term for a black, it was, here, originally, an attempt to describe the dancing ragtime rhythm by comparing it with the Irish jig.) This was the syncopated piano music that Joplin, along with the others, was playing, as it gradually crystallized into a distinct musical form.

It was an historic, if inevitably clandestine, meeting of two cultures. If, in the ragtime form, the elements of scale, key, and harmony (and the instrument itself) came from the white side, the crucial, catalytic polyrhythms came from the black.

Although ragtime was melodious, it was the exciting rhythm of its melodies that was so novel and so instantly appealing. To understand what took place in ragtime it is necessary to go back to earlier black-American music and its retentions from African music. Polyrhythm, with or without drums, is the *sine qua non* of African native music. In Black America, from the first work-songs of slavery on, duple and triple polyrhythms persisted as a basic practice. Without drums (which were eventually forbidden) they issued from the appositions of hand-clapping, foot-stamping, or the sounds of tools, and the sung melodic line. The first factor, regularly accented, formed a basic ostinato. The chant or melody (like the improvising drum in an African battery) was free to wander from the strong beats to the weak, to delay or to anticipate, to drop unpredictably between beats, and even to pose an odd meter to the even (e.g., 3/4 phrasing over 4/4). It was a drama of tensions: a rhythmic base of metric affirmation, and a melody of metric denial.

Ragtime's polyrhythms came from the right

hand's phrasings in syncope, or between the beat, or in variant meter above a regularly accented 2/4 or 4/4 bass. Ragtime pioneer Ben Harney called it "playing two different times at once."[5] It had come about with the first free generation of self-taught black pianists' playing quadrilles and, particularly, improvising piano transcriptions of the extremely popular brass band marches. Early ragtime publications, in fact, usually carry the designation: *Tempo di marcia.*

In 1971, the octogenarian ragtime composer Eubie Blake (born in 1883) recalled the early eastern ragtime "march kings," particularly one William Turk (born about the same time as Scott Joplin), who had "a left hand like God," and a certain "One-Leg" Willie Joseph, a conservatory-trained black ragtimer who would "bring the house down with *The Stars and Stripes Forever* in march time, ragtime, and 'sixteen' " (*TAPR* 193), the latter meaning a fast boogie-woogie bass.

Ragtime's structural form likewise points to beginnings in syncopated march playing. The typical Sousa march contains four to five themes, generally, in two or more keys. Each theme as a rule is sixteen measures long and is usually repeated. The piano rag takes a similar form, most often with four themes. As ragtime developed it added an interesting device, that of habitually reprising the first theme immediately after the second theme. Whether this was a kind of conscious or unconscious reference to rondo form is not known.

Considering the degree to which piano playing in the red-light areas was either song or dance accompaniment or, at the other extreme, merely background music, it is rather remarkable that the separate ragtime piece ever developed at all. It is a measure of the talent and aims of a small number of the honky-tonk coterie that they should have wanted to progress from the tempting easefulness of the whole situation. They insisted on an audience; composed for it; and then—a few of

them—insisted on the publication of their work.

To them we owe the ragtime form, a delightful concision with enough themes (albeit without development) for a larger form. The classic piano rag is an ivory miniature among the large canvases. When the rag began to take shape in the early to mid-1890s, Scott Joplin became its special master.

Just as it was all beginning, he arrived in St Louis. It was 1885. Though only seventeen, Joplin was already an experienced musician. St Louis, which had been a trading post for the French-Canadian *voyageurs* in their dugout canoes, was still in spirit a frontier town. It sprawled and brawled along the levees in this penultimate time of the great riverboat era. The Mississippi, still a great trade and travel artery, was thick with traffic. Its air echoed with the sound of chanteys mingling with the levee-camp blues, and the blasts and drone of steamboat whistles blending with the singing of roustabouts "coonjining" to the plunking banjos.

In St Louis money grew not on trees but on the river. The easy silver dollars spawned one of the most wide-open "Districts" in the country. Centering around two ill-famed streets, Chestnut and Market, were the saloons and cafés, the pool halls and the bawdy "parlors," all ringing with syncopated piano. "Jig piano" was everywhere. During the next eight years or so it would come of age, a development that would center mainly here and in another Missouri city, Sedalia.

Joplin now made St Louis the only remotely stable center of a still nomadic life. His base of operations became "Honest John" Turpin's Silver Dollar saloon, which was a ragtime clubhouse, battleground of musical duels, and informal booking office for the youthful piano cult. A madam would send a girl over: "We have company now and need a professor." They would match coins and someone had a job.

Joplin was never very far away, playing at Hannibal or Columbia, at Carthage, Jefferson City, or Sedalia; just across the river in East St Louis, or perhaps as far as Cincinnati or Louisville.

In 1893 the World's Columbian Exposition,

---

5   Rudi Blesh and Harriet Janis *They All Played Ragtime* (New York: Oak Publications 1971)—hereafter, abbreviated in the text: *TAPR.*

popularly known as the Chicago World's Fair, was opened after having been postponed for a year. The ragtime fraternity convened there, along the Fair's amusement "Midway" and in the Chicago Tenderloin, which ran from Eighteenth Street to the Illinois Central railroad tracks. It was a bonanza for ragtimers.

Joplin formed a small orchestra in which he doubled on piano and cornet, and got a steady job in the District. Off hours he, like the others, repaired to the favorite hangout, pianist Johnny Seymour's Bar, where a national rather than a regional meeting and comparing of individual styles took place, both informally and in public ragtime contests. A fluid, fugitive music was being crystallized. The many catchy little sixteen-bar themes, invented almost at random by a footloose, talented young generation, began to be assembled in the A-B-A-C-D form, beholden to rondo, quadrille, and military march.

At the Fair's end in the autumn, Joplin returned to St Louis, stopped there briefly, and then went on to Sedalia, where he settled down for the better part of a year, becoming a part of respectable black society. He joined the Queen City Concert Band as second cornetist, sang with vocal quartets, and played the piano at social gatherings. He was now beginning to compose—songs, piano waltzes and marches—but not yet (so far as is known) in ragtime form.

Although it was a pleasant scene and one, beyond doubt, more congenial to Scott Joplin's essentially sober nature than the red-light milieu, he nevertheless soon wandered back to St Louis. The Rosebud Cafe on Market Street was now the ragtime haven. It was run by "Honest John's" son, Thomas Million Turpin, a heavy, hulking man, blunt in manner, but noted for his warm, generous hospitality. A player and composer himself, he had huge, agile hands and a humorous, rather athletic, ragtime style. Within three years from this time—in 1897—he would become the first Negro to publish a rag. He was host, pace-setter, and confidant of a gifted group of young black players that included Louis Chauvin, Charles

Warfield, Sam Patterson, Artie Matthews, Joe Jordan, Charlie Thompson, and Rob Hampton. Mostly teenagers (Joplin was now twenty-six), they met at all hours at the Rosebud, and a little later at Turpin's Hurrah Sporting Club in an alley at the rear. In the Rosebud it was the wine room in the back, "accessible from the bar or through the side 'family entrance' . . . where the sports and the girls gathered. . . . This room was the rendezvous for every St Louis or visiting pianist. The hottest sessions, however, witnessed only by the musicians themselves, generally took place in the parlor of Mother Johnson's house across the street" (*TAPR* 54). For three or four hours there would be a "cutting contest," purely pianistic, between a St Louis representative and, say, a visitor from New York.

FIRST PUBLICATIONS

It was an exciting scene but by late 1895 Joplin was back in Sedalia. Though not completely weaned from nomadism, his concept of the nature and purpose of the wandering life had seemingly changed. Despite appearances he may have had a general sense of direction even when taking leave from Texarkana. He formed the Texas Medley Quartette (actually an octet of male singers) which included his younger brothers Will and Robert, who had moved to Sedalia, and embarked on a professional tour. Scott Joplin conducted; sang solos; and—most important of all—began writing songs for their repertory as well as his own piano solos. After tryouts in Sedalia the Medley Quartette got vaudeville bookings that took them that year (1895) as far as Syracuse, New York. There Joplin sold his first pieces for publication to two local music stores: Leiter Bros published *A Picture of Her Face,* and M. L. Mantell issued *Please Say You Will.*

There are no intimations of genius in Scott Joplin's first publications. *A Picture of Her Face* is a Victorian mourning picture in sound, designed for male quartet rendition and wholly undistinguished. The other song, though more cheerful, is equally run-of-the-mill.

In 1896 the Quartette toured Louisiana and Texas. In Temple, Texas, Joplin secured his first piano publications: *Combination March* and *Harmony Club Waltz,* both with the local imprint of Robert Smith; and *The (Great) Crush Collision March,* published by John R. Fuller.

The first two numbers are uneventful period pieces. *Crush Collision March,* however, is a period piece of a special sort. As much program music as a march, it is, strangely, "Dedicated to the M. K. & T. Ry.," this being the Missouri, Kansas and Texas Railway, which runs through Temple and there crosses the tracks of another line. The march describes a train wreck that, quite possibly, had recently occurred (otherwise why the dedication?). Could there have been a wreck at the crossing in Temple? And could Joplin have added sound-effects and descriptive narrative to a piece already written but unpublished? Or had he quickly composed a work to fit the situation?

Topical or not, and with all its bombast, *The (Great) Crush Collision March* is a multi-theme piece with the trio constituting a descriptive section that abounds in musical sound-effects. Speed is conveyed by treble chords over a rapid chromatic bass, with the narrative printed between the staves: "The noise of the trains while running at the rate of sixty miles per hour." Then: "Whistling for the crossing," with piercing discords; then "The train noise," followed once more by "Whistle before the collision," conveyed by even more frantic discords higher up. Then comes "The Collision," a crashing fortissimo chord in the bass.

Crush Collision March is chiefly interesting in the Joplin story because parts of it may have been an early essay in ragtime. The evidence for this is chiefly to be found in the second and third themes which, although printed in regular, "square" meter, almost beg to be syncopated. That they may have been played that way but printed otherwise is not surprising. In its very beginnings ragtime publication faced a difficult hurdle: commercial arrangers didn't know how to notate it and publishers shunned it as strange and hard to play.

After the ice was broken with the first ragtime publications in 1897, the better ragtime composers still suffered from the publishers' arbitrary practice of simplifying difficult scores into more tractable, salable versions. Years later, Scott Joplin, having himself suffered from this practice, was to write in his instruction manual, *School of Ragtime,* of the difficulties of playing "real ragtime."

In 1897 the Texas Medley Quartette ended its second and final tour in Joplin, Missouri, and then disbanded. Scott went to work briefly in the red-light district that clustered around the House of Lords, before returning to Sedalia to settle back easily into the community. Not yet thirty years old, he would seem to have set his future course, at least in his own mind. An already mature man of marked reserve, he was nevertheless a magnetic person whose dynamism was doubly effective for its quietness. There is no reason to doubt that he had already formed the radical concept of a classic ragtime worthy of being seriously accepted and perpetuated in published scores. From his own reliably reported statements we know that he finished his most famous piece, the *Maple Leaf Rag,* in 1897, two years before it was published; also we know what he thought of it. An associate, the white player Brun Campbell, known as "The Ragtime Kid," recalled:

> When I bade Scott Joplin good-by as I left for my home in Kansas in 1899, he gave me a bright new silver half-dollar dated 1897 and calling my attention to the date said: "Carry this for good luck and remember that it is dated the year that I finished my first rag." As he handed it to me he had a very strange and sad expression in his eyes. I have never forgotten that look. (*TAPR* 29)

Another and closer associate, the young Sedalian Arthur Marshall, related that when the piece was first completed and written down, Joplin said to him: "Arthur, the *Maple Leaf* will make me King of Ragtime Composers" (*TAPR* 33).

Now in 1896, back in Sedalia, wandering was

over. A settled, quiet purposiveness took its place. Though the inequities of the Negro's position there, as everywhere in America, forced Joplin to work in the honky-tonk fringe of the Tenderloin, he conducted his private life elsewhere. He went to live for a few months in the family home of Arthur Marshall, then a fifteen-year-old ragtime neophyte. Simultaneously he became Arthur's college mate at the George R. Smith College for Negroes operated by the Methodist Church. Joplin enrolled in courses in harmony and composition to supplement his elementary childhood training in Texarkana and the pragmatic music education he had acquired in his travels.

He quickly became the center of Sedalia's black musical life. The whole varied group of pioneering ragtimers—from the older honky-tonk hands like Otis Saunders, Jim Hastings, and A. Chestine to youths like Marshall and the fourteen-year-old Scott Hayden, a student at Lincoln High—gathered around him. It was largely Joplin who effected the drastic change in attitude of Sedalia's proper, church-going black society. With a quiet, decent man like him playing in dubious Main Street haunts like the Maple Leaf Club, these purlieus and their syncopated "sinful" music began to seem less disreputable. When one considers the deeply ingrained prejudices involved, it was extraordinary that Joplin was able to move so freely between respectable world and underworld.

It was a crucial period for black music which in 1896 was taking a definitive, potentially classic, but quite possibly ephemeral, shape in an unsanctioned world. Limited to improvisation and a few perishable, unpublished scores, it might well have continued for a few years more and then have disappeared forever. Fortunately there were personalities and forces sufficient to contravene such an end. While classic ragtime was flowering at the Rosebud around Tom Turpin and at the Maple Leaf Club around Scott Joplin, there were a few white men becoming interested and involved. There is no denying the brutal fact: at that time, without white concern and capital, ragtime was lost. Practically speaking, were it to survive with enough time for full fruition, it needed to be heard throughout white America and it needed to be preserved in printed scores.

In April 1896 the first of these steps was negotiated. A young Kentuckian, Benjamin Robertson Harney, introduced ragtime as "jig piano" on the stage at Tony Pastor's Theatre on the New York Rialto. An immediate, resounding hit, it was the indispensable initial breakthrough to the white world—the white world, that is, that included wives as well as husbands. Within months, coupled with a craze for the concomitant Negro social dance called the cakewalk, ragtime became a nationwide craze.

Meanwhile, Joplin and other black rag writers were striving for publication. He offered his *Maple Leaf Rag* soon after completing it to the Sedalia music house of A. W. Perry & Son and was turned down. Then, less than nine months after the Harney debut, came the first piano rag publication. A white band leader of Chicago, William H. Krell, secured a publisher for his *Mississippi Rag*, which was copyrighted on January 27 1897.

At the turn of the century, the only mechanical music of any consequence was the player piano with its slotted paper rolls and foot-pumped pneumatic action activating the keys. Movies were mute. The early Edison cylinder graphophone was quite accurately called the "talking machine." The music in the American home was made there and—aside from the player piano—was played and sung "live." A piano (or reed organ) was almost as indispensable as a television set or stereo playback is in 1971. Sheet music was paramount, tied in with its exploitation in vaudeville, café, and music store. It is scarcely an exaggeration to say that the appearance in sheet music of a new music hit by a new writer was then as important as a television premiere in the 1970s.

So it was that *Mississippi Rag* opened the floodgates for what would soon be a deluge of ragtime publications. That the opener was by a white composer may reveal our racial priorities but it by no means implies that ragtime itself was of white origin. Though its cover bears the untrue blurb,

"The First Rag-Time Two-Step Ever Written," its picture of black dancers coonjining on a levee to the syncopating banjos implicitly acknowledges the true origins of the music.

In December 1897 Tom Turpin with his *Harlem Rag* became the first of the black ragtime originators to be published. After his turndown by Perry, Joplin seems to have concentrated mostly on composing. There is no evidence that he saw John Stark at this time. Stark owned Sedalia's other music store and had already taken a flyer in publishing with a few inconsequential songs.

It was the end of 1898 before Joplin went to the publisher Carl Hoffman in Kansas City carrying several completed rags in manuscript. Encouraged by his arranger, Hoffman bought a piece called *Original Rags* but passed up the *Maple Leaf Rag*. Three months later, in March 1899, *Original Rags* appeared. The cover portrays an old plantation Negro picking up rags in front of a ramshackle cabin; under the title are the words: "Picked by Scott Joplin—Arranged by Chas. N. Daniels."

This rather quippy subtitle has been interpreted as meaning that Scott Joplin did not compose this rag but "picked" themes then current in the public-domain ragtime world; and that Daniels arranged the music for him.

Neither of these beliefs seems to be well-founded. The inscription, first of all, is a would-be-humorous or deprecatory allusion to the intrinsically belittling term "ragtime." It is part and parcel of the blackface-minstrel ethos: a double pun, first on the activities of a rag (or junk) picker, and second, on the then-new slang term for ragtime playing: "picking the piano," which of course derives from the archaic banjo-picking ragtime days. As to the music, it is unmistakably Joplin; the credit to Daniels would appear to have been the publisher's way of acknowledging his help in recommending it for publication. Daniels, incidentally, later became a successful composer in his own right, achieving considerable fame under the name of Neil Moret. By 1901 he had a hit of national proportions in his *Hiawatha—A Summer Idyl*.

Scott Joplin's apprenticeship was now far behind him. *Original Rags* is a fine and realized piece, able to stand with his whole subsequent publication of more than two-score piano works: rags, marches, waltzes, and a tango. The *Original Rags* themes are mutually sympathetic and adroitly combined; its melodies are strongly and personally Joplinesque; its combination of off-center treble with regularly accented *ostinato* bass has a formidable "swing" (it was then called "ragginess"). Though appearing early in ragtime history, it is formally realized.

Original Rags is both typical and atypical of the characteristic piano rag form which, as we have noted, usually combines four sixteen-measure themes in 2/4 or 4/4 meter, generally as follows: Introduction; A-A-B-B-A; transition; C-C-D-D; *codetta*. The four- to eight-bar introduction is usual; the short transition is rare and usually used in modulation; the *codetta* (or "tag") is fairly rare. The basic rag schema is comprised in the 144 measures of the four themes arranged as shown—although it should be re-emphasized that this arrangement is typical, not mandatory, and the variants are many. In all of them, however, the repeats, too often disregarded in performance, are essential to the symmetry and completeness of the form.

The original meter is generally maintained throughout but, besides the usual 2/4 and occasional 4/4 there are 6/8 march-rags and 3/4 syncopated rag-waltzes. The tempo as set at the beginning was—from Joplin's day—held all through. The functional use of ragtime to accompany marching and dancing (the cake walk was both in one) insured a fixed tempo, just as minuet and gavotte were so governed in their day. Nevertheless, not only is *rubato* implicit in classic ragtime (and most particularly so with Joplin), but *ritardandi* and *accelerandi* in melodic turns and in cadences seem so obviously pertinent that they are an accepted part of serious ragtime playing today.

The themes may be in one key and mode but often in two or three keys (generally in a tonic, dominant, subdominant relationship) and, with

Joplin, may involve contrasting minor themes.

Though Joplin in general adhered to the basic A-A-B-B-A-C-C-D-D sequence, it is interesting that his first and final rags do not. *Original Rags,* like the posthumously published valedictory of 1917, *Reflection Rag,* features five themes. In *Original Rags* the schema also delays reentry of the first theme: Introduction; A-A-B-B-C-C; modulation; A-D-D-E-E.

Apart from technical observations, *Original Rags* is a charming and auspicious beginning to the life work of the master ragtime composer. Appearing early in 1899 it was to lead, before the year's end, to the rag that is the cornerstone of Joplin's ragtime *oeuvre.* The *Maple Leaf Rag* brought its composer almost instant fame, enabled him to retire once and for all from the underworld, and confirmed his own prophecy: it made him "The King of Ragtime Composers."

The publication of *Original Rags,* important as it was to Joplin, was but one incident in an active life. In 1899 in Sedalia, when not playing publicly, he was composing or teaching. He helped Arthur Marshall and Scott Hayden to complete their first ragtimes essays: *Swipesy Cake Walk* and *Sunflower Slow Drag.* Joplin was encouraging his two teenage Sedalia protegés to compose, was helping them to arrange and write out their material, and himself writing themes to fill out their conceptions— all to assist them in getting publication. When the actual publications appeared they bore joint composer credits.

MAPLE LEAF RAG

Although creatively far ahead of his time and place, Joplin was also imprisoned in it. Beyond the publishing of piano rags and, perhaps, money and a certain circumscribed fame, where, in America, could he go? Even in Sedalia he was limited to the black world or the tolerance—and exile—of the Tenderloin. If his conceptions were those of genius, still his genius wore a black skin. To realize his expanding visions and, with them, to reach out to a wider world, he needed a white advocate.

Scott Joplin found that advocate and more, a friend as well as champion, in a fellow Sedalian. John Stillwell Stark was a generation older than Joplin. Born in 1841 in Shelby County, Kentucky, of early American stock, Stark was the eleventh child of a family of twelve. His mother died—in that final childbirth—when he was three, and he was only six when an older brother emigrated with him on horseback to stake out a homestead in Indiana.

John lived on the farm and did rough field work. He got his log-cabin schooling during the days when the star of a country lawyer named Abraham Lincoln was rising and the conscience of the North was becoming more and more troubled by "The Peculiar Institution," slavery.

John Stark was, and all his life continued to be, a pioneer in attitude and in act. After serving the Blue during the Civil War, he married a thirteen-year-old New Orleans girl, a pretty little praline vendor named Sarah Ann Casey, took her North, sent her to school, took a homestead in Missouri, and began to raise a family. By 1872 there were three children: two sons, Etilmon and William, and a daughter, Eleanor.

By 1880 he had gone from pioneer farming on to pioneering in the then new ice cream business, making his own product and selling it through the countryside from a Conestoga covered wagon. Soon, pioneering again, he was carrying a reed organ for sale along with the ice cream. Success in peddling these harmoniums eased him into the music business. In 1885 he moved from Chillicothe eighty miles south to the bustling railroad center, Sedalia. There, with his younger son, Will, he set up a music store. In the years that followed, the music house of John Stark & Son planted itself firmly into the local scene.

Soon Stark and his talented family were at the focus of white musical life in Sedalia as Scott Joplin and his two youthful protegés were on the black side. Stark's elder son Etilmon, a violinist, became a bandleader and music instructor at the local military academy, and daughter Eleanor (or

Nell) was doing so well at the piano that she would soon be sent abroad to study with Moritz Moszkowski. Musical soirées were held at the Stark store and, on occasional summer nights, Sedalians were treated to serenades. An 1894 item in the *Sedalia Gazette* described one of these evening musical treats, with Miss Nellie Stark as one of the performers (*TAPR* 49).

Five years later another pleasant musical event would decisively alter the lives of two men, one black and one white: Scott Joplin and John Stark. What began as a casual musical moment proved to be one of the first shots of the Ragtime Revolution.

It was the summer of 1899. Stark, already a grizzled, bearded man of fifty-eight, dropped into the Maple Leaf Club on Main Street for a cool beer. "Quaffing the brew," as one said in those days, he heard syncopated music coming from the upright piano at the rear. He listened: though his daughter might play Liszt and he might approve, he himself, nurtured on folk music, was incorrigibly native. He listened and then, schooner in hand, strolled over. A black man was playing a rag. One by one its four themes rippled out over the striding bass. By the time the first theme had reappeared, Stark was tapping his foot and smiling. The player looked up and nodded his head in greeting.

When the piece came to an end, Stark said: "Hello, Joplin. That's a good number. Is it yours?" Assured that it was, he asked the composer to drop in next day at the Stark store. Joplin came, the *Maple Leaf Rag* conquered, and John Stark bought it for fifty dollars with an arrangement for a continuing royalty to Joplin.

That is the story of how it began as told a half-century later by one of Joplin's Sedalia friends, Tom Ireland, who had played clarinet with the Queen City Concert Band with which Joplin had once played cornet.[6]

What happened the next day was related still later by Mrs Will Stark, John Stark's daughter-

in-law. As Carrie Bruggeman she had been a song plugger in a St Louis department store when Will met her after the Starks had moved to St Louis and several years after the publication of *Maple Leaf Rag*. In 1961, a dozen years after Will Stark's death, his widow gave the following account:

> According to Will . . . Joplin wandered into the Stark store in Sedalia one day holding the *Maple Leaf Rag* manuscript in one hand, and a little boy's hand with the other. Sitting down at the piano, Joplin began to play the now-famous tune while the youngster stepped it off. Grandpa (John Stark) thought nobody would play it because it was too difficult . . . but Will was so taken with the lad's dance, that he decided to buy it.[7]

One might venture to doubt that Will, rather than John Stark, was making the decisions. On the other hand, one might believe that Joplin did bring along a little dancer. That he was deeply fascinated by the close ties between dancing and ragtime is seen in the work he was then composing, *The Ragtime Dance*.

EXPANDING VISIONS

As the *Maple Leaf Rag* neared publication in September 1899, Joplin was busy preparing *The Ragtime Dance* for a public performance. Although there were precedents for the style and format of his piano rags, this new work represented a strikingly original concept: a kind of ragtime ballet based on Negro social dances of the time, with sung narration.

The Ragtime Dance was Joplin's journey-piece on his way to full-length opera. In the introductory section the vocalist sets the scene for an elegant ball. Five dance themes follow, each one repeated, with each repeated section calling for a different dance step, during which the singer acts as the caller of the figures. The dancers are directed to execute now-forgotten dance

---

6 Conversation with Rudi Blesh and Harriet Janis, in Sedalia, October 26 1949.

7 Interview with Dorothy Brockhoff, St Louis *Post-Dispatch* in January 1961.

steps: Ragtime Dance, Clean Up Dance, Jennie Cooler Dance, Slow Drag, World's Fair Dance, Back Step Prance, Dude Walk, Sedidus Walk, Town Talk, and the minstrel-show dance specialty Stop Time, in which strong beats and tacets are marked by foot stamping.

Late in 1899 Joplin rented the Woods Opera House in Sedalia for a single night. *The Ragtime Dance* was performed there by four dancing couples, with Will Joplin as vocalist, and the composer conducting a ragtime orchestra from the piano. The orchestration had cost many weeks of work, with faithful Arthur Marshall painstakingly copying the parts.

The Stark family was invited, the expressed hope being that John Stark would publish the work. With the *Maple Leaf* so recently published and only just beginning to catch on, it was patently too early to approach Stark with so ambitious a project. While he did not turn it down, the matter was shelved for the time being.

Shortly after this the *Maple Leaf Rag* began to take hold. First it sold out in Sedalia. Then outside inquiries began coming in. Stark moved to set up sales contacts, first throughout Missouri, then regionally, then nationwide. The first great instrumental sheet music hit in America was happening: sales snowballed, moving in the first six months or so toward the first 75,000 copies. Eventually it would top the million mark. It has long since moved out of the "hit" class: hits fade, but *Maple Leaf* has become an American institution. It is still in print and still popular.

Where *Original Rags* is the essence of folk dance-song, the *Maple Leaf Rag* is alive with announcement and expectation, a prelude in the musical sense of the term: a curtain seems to rise with its abrupt ascending *arpeggio*. And a true prelude the *Maple Leaf* was, in the lives of composer and publisher and, in a wider sense, as the curtain-raiser for the phenomenal development of classic ragtime that immediately ensued. It was, to perfection, the archetype. For at least a dozen years a large proportion of published rags consciously or unconsciously followed

the metric patterns or melodic lines of Joplin's prototype, or else had variants or new melodies based on its harmonic progressions.

Toward the end of the summer of 1900, Stark moved his business to St Louis. The *Maple Leaf Rag* dictated and financed the move. For a short while Stark and son ran off hurried copies in a hotel room on a rented hand press. These hurried copies helped to pay for a printing plant on Laclede Avenue. Then the voluminous copies from the plant bought a family home for the Starks on Washington Boulevard. A labor shift was added; father and son took off their overalls, donned blue serge, and moved into offices. Other rags began to be issued, the first of which was the Joplin-Marshall collaboration, *Swipesy—Cake Walk*. It was an auspicious start for a fifty-nine-year-old ex-soldier, ex-farmer, ex-ice cream manufacturer, ex-music store owner in a new business in a new city at what was then considered an advanced age. Some years later, in his seventies, Stark wrote, with his wry, persimmon-puckered humor: "There is an impression that old men should be chloroformed at sixty."[8]

Scott Joplin followed right after Stark. Just before leaving Sedalia he married Belle Hayden, Scott Hayden's widowed sister-in-law. They found a house in St Louis at 2658-A Morgan Street, where they would remain for three years. Joplin now concentrated completely on teaching and composing. With the added income from *Maple Leaf* royalties he abandoned all further activity in the sporting world. Now, during his occasional calls at the Rosebud, he was a visitor, not a competitor for the parlor jobs. His friendships with Turpin and the younger men like Louis Chauvin and Sam Patterson remained unchanged. Added financial security came when Mrs Joplin converted their residence into a professional boarding and rooming house

In March 1901, with Stark caught up on production, three new Joplin works were published:

8 Quoted in *TAPR* (52) from Axel Christensen's *Ragtime Review*.

Peacherine Rag, Augustan Club Waltzes, and a collaboration with Hayden, *Sunflower Slow Drag. Sunflower* is among the early gems of ragtime. The musical rapport demonstrated here, as in the Joplin-Marshall *Swipesy,* indicates the generous relationship that Joplin could establish with other talents. Blithely ignoring Hayden, however, Stark wrote the blurb for *Sunflower* in his characteristically flamboyant style:

> This piece came to light during the high temperature of Scott Joplin's courtship, and while he was touching the ground only in the highest places, his geese were all swans, and the Mississippi water tasted like honey-dew . . . . If there ever was a song without words, this is that article: hold your ear to the ground while someone plays it, and you can hear Scott Joplin's heart beat. (*TAPR* 53)

Seven months passed before the next rag appeared. *The Easy Winners,* a captivatingly melodious piece, was Joplin's first publication of one of his own works. Why Stark did not issue *Easy Winners* is not clear, but it shows that Joplin could hardly (as some believe) have signed an exclusive five-year contract with him at the time he had bought *Maple Leaf.* The existence of such a contract has never been confirmed by Stark's descendants.

Joplin, meanwhile, continued his efforts to persuade Stark to publish *The Ragtime Dance.* He decided to present it again, this time for the Starks alone in a private hall. Nell Stark, just returned from her European studies, talked her father into publishing the much-mooted work. It was finally issued in 1902 and its extremely meager sales bore out Stark's reservations about publishing it.

The publication came at the very end of the year, together with three more Joplin works: *A Breeze From Alabama, Elite Syncopations,* and *The Entertainer.* Shortly before this, in addition, Stark had issued Joplin's *March Majestic* and *The Strenuous Life.* Nor were the six Stark issues all that Joplin had published in this fertile year. In April the Thiebes-Stierlin Music Co had published a song, *I Am Thinking of My Pickaninny*

Days and a month later S. Simon released *Cleopha.*

Though the song bears the date MCMI it was not copyrighted (nor, presumably, issued) until 1902. The first Joplin song to appear since 1895, it is a folkish melody somewhat in the Stephen Foster vein but essentially a sentimental potboiler. Worse: by today's standards the lyrics, written by Henry Jackson, are studded with objectionable terms like "pickaninny" and "darkey," and present the false notion that the old plantation days were a happy Eden for Negroes.

Cleopha, subtitled *March and Two-Step,* is very much a march in character but with spicy syncopations. It almost immediately became a favorite of the Sousa band. The brass band idiom also determines the overall character of *A Breeze From Alabama.*

1902 is notable for the appearance of *The Entertainer.* Its beguiling melodies are as sunny as any that Joplin ever wrote, their frank, open folklike quality artfully concealing a fastidious art. *The Entertainer* was dedicated to James Brown and his Mandolin Club and indeed some of its melodies recall the pluckings and the fast tremolos of the little steel-stringed plectrum instruments that were once so popular. At the turn of the century, mandolin orchestras of fifty pieces —eight-, ten-, and twelve-string mandolins with mando-cello and mando-bass or *guitarron*—were not unknown. Far more common, however, were the small wandering string groups called "serenaders." Combining guitars, mandolins, fiddles, and string bass, they played ragtime, waltzes, and popular ballads in the streets. Invited indoors, they might join with the piano.

In 1903 Joplin bought a thirteen-room house in a good neighborhood on Lucas Avenue. The St. Louis city directory of that year listed him as music teacher, an inadequate description of a life mostly given to composing. As the year progressed, Joplin's relations with John Stark became strained, largely because of the commercial failure of *The Ragtime Dance.* It was already becoming apparent to Stark that his star composer was not going to remain content with writing only short (and readily salable) piano rags; he knew that Joplin already was well along in composing a ragtime opera and that he was counting on him to publish it.

The situation had the makings of an impasse. Although there was mutual good will, each man, according to his lights, was right. Joplin's natural concern was to develop his art and to have his works published and performed. His imagination, which had long ago overtaken other ragtime writers, was now threatening to leave Stark behind as well. As Stark saw the matter, just to publish fine piano rags and propagandize them (as he was ably and vividly doing) seemed a revolutionary thing in itself. He staunchly believed in ragtime as he knew it. But it appeared doubtful that he could make the giant leap of faith from piano rags to ragtime ballet, opera—and who knows?—even symphony.

Joplin, however, saw it not as a leap but as a logical development. He would go on believing this until he died. Few if any in America had similar vision and faith. The picture was considerably clearer to open minds elsewhere, away from the moralistic and racial prejudices that distorted and inhibited our acceptance of a native art.

The enlightened European view of the American cultural scene in that period was well expressed by Arnold Bennett in 1913.[9] Unequivocally he wrote that "ragtime is absolutely characteristic of its inventors—from nowhere but the United States could such music have sprung. . . . Nor can there be any doubt about its vigour, brimming over with life. . . . Here for those who have ears to hear are the seeds from which a national art may ultimately spring." But Bennett had scant faith that our ears *would* hear. "The American dilettanti," he said, "never did and never will look in the right quarters for vital art. A really original artist struggling under their very noses has small chance of being recognized by them, the reason being that they are imitative with no real opinions of their own. They associate art with Florentine frames, matinée hats, distant museums, and clever talk full of allusions to the dead. It would not occur to them to search for American art in the architecture of railway stations and the draughtsmanship and sketch-writing of newspapers, because they have not the wit to learn that genuine art flourishes best in the atmosphere of genuine public demand."

Bennett made no big thing of pedigree or sanctions. "The sole test of a musical public," he continued, "is that it should be capable of self-support. I mean that it should produce a school of creative and executive artists of its own, whom it likes well enough to idolize and enrich, and whom the rest of the world will respect."

Almost as Bennett was writing, the influential magazine *Musical America* was complaining that ragtime "exalts noise, rush, and street vulgarity. It suggests repulsive dance-halls and restaurants."[10] (*Musical America* was far too refined even to hint at bordellos in the offing!)

This was the chilly, official side of the home climate that John Stark felt. The problem was simple enough: He was a "realist"; Scott Joplin was an artist. As the situation developed, a New York popular composer, Monroe H. Rosenfeld, doing an article on Joplin in a St Louis newspaper, reported:

Joplin's ambition is to shine in other spheres . . . . To this end he is assiduously toiling upon an opera, nearly a score of the numbers of which he has already composed and which he hopes to give an early production [in] this city.[11]

Despite his concentration on *A Guest of Honor*, the opera in question, Joplin had ready, or was completing, several new rags, none of which were brought out by Stark. The Val A. Reis Music Company of St Louis issued *Weeping Willow* and also a new Joplin-Hayden collaboration, *Something Doing;* the Chicago house of Victor

9   *The Times* (London) February 8 1913.

10   *Musical America* (March 29 1913).
11   St Louis *Globe-Democrat* (June 7 1903).

Kremer published *Palm Leaf Rag;* a song *Little Black Baby,* copyrighted by one Louise Armstrong Bristol and published by Success Music Company, Chicago, completed the year's output.

The 1903 rags are prevailingly songlike; even the rhythmic *Something Doing* has a beautifully flowing second subject. In *Weeping Willow* the trio—frequently a strongly rhythmic section in Joplin's rags—continues the flowing *cantilena.* The variety in the composer's melodic concepts is evident if one compares *Weeping Willow* and *Palm Leaf Rag.* The first is like particularly graceful folk song; the melodies of the second, no less graceful, are song sublimated for the sophisticated music salon. *Little Black Baby,* on the other hand, must be dismissed as an unfortunate potboiler, difficult to reconcile with Joplin's usual good taste. It would seem to have been fitted to order to an excruciatingly coy text by a lady amateur lyrics-writer and published at her expense (the copyright is in her name) by a "vanity press." The cover design shows a photograph of a white—not black—baby, but omits Joplin's name, which is just as well.

Joplin himself was guilty on occasion of writing vocal texts that contained objectionable terms, but of a different and more significant kind. The use of expressions like "coon," "razor fight," and "dark town," found in the opening section of *The Ragtime Dance,* for instance, illustrates a shameful convention that was accepted—then and for a long time to come—by black and white. In Joplin's time the vanguard poet Paul Laurence Dunbar could write:

> But hit's Sousa played in rag-time, an' hit's Rastus
>   on Parade,
> W'en de colo'd ban' comes ma'chin' down de
>   street.[12]

And on into the 1930s the greatest of all blues singers, Bessie Smith, who could unflinchingly indict white exploitation of black in *Poor Man's Blues,* could also sing:

> Check your razors and your guns:
>   We'll be 'rasslin' when the wagon comes. . . .[13]

But there was also black pride in Dunbar's poem and in Bessie's music.

Joplin's obsessive drive towards completing, staging, and getting publication for the opera *A Guest of Honor* threw the Starks into a state of confusion. Stark descendants have related that the opera was a family topic for years, a project initially embraced, then postponed, then planned again, but never accomplished. For one thing, they wanted Joplin to write a stronger book and, apparently, he never did.

The story of Scott Joplin's first opera not only is a sad story but also a nagging, unsolved mystery entangled in a web of rumors. For what little is known of the presumably only public performance (although it is rumored also to have been done once in Sedalia), we must again rely upon Marshall:

> As for the Rag Time Opera, *A Guest of Honor* was performed once in St. Louis. In a large hall where they often gave dances. It was a test-out or dress rehearsal to get the idea of the public sentiment. It was taken quite well and I think [Joplin] was about to get Haviland or Majestic Producers to handle or finance the play, also book it. I can't say just how far it got—as I was very eager for greater money, I left St. Louis for Chicago. (*TAPR* 71)

It was never booked, performed again, nor published. There are rumors (not too fanciful to be true) that Joplin later published some of its numbers as separate rags. If so, their identity is not known. At the time, anyway, Scott Joplin's first major project had become a major frustration.

Nor is this all. Here begins the unsolved mystery: what became of the book and score? In 1946 the late Roy Carew, an early and ardent Joplinophile, looking through the files of the Copyright Office in Washington, found a card with the notation: "A GUEST OF HONOR, a

---

12 *The Complete Poems of Paul Laurence Dunbar* (New York: Dodd, Mead & Co 1896, 1913) 286-287.

13 *Gimme a Pigfoot and a Bottle of Beer* on the Columbia recording (CL 856) *The Bessie Smith Story,* Vol 2.

ragtime opera, written and composed by Scott Joplin. Entered in the name of Scott Joplin, under C 42461, Feb. 18, 1903." He also reported the further notation: "Copies never received." All traces of the original manuscript have vanished, but even as late as the early 1950s there were people still living who remembered the opera and its beautiful raggy music.

As to its whereabouts, what had started as conjecture soon developed into unlikely rumors and far-fetched clues. Lottie Stokes Joplin, Scott's second wife, whom he married later in New York, had no knowledge of what had become of score or book. She ventured a tentative opinion in 1949 (thirty-two years after Joplin's death) that the missing material might, *just might,* have been in a trunk full of Joplin's clothing, unpublished music, letters, and family photographs, that Joplin, she said, had left against an unpaid bill in a theatrical rooming house in Pittsburgh. This would have occurred not long before their marriage when, between 1907 and 1909, Joplin was intermittently out on vaudeville tours. The trunk, Mrs Joplin said, had never been reclaimed, nor could she give an address for the rooming house.

Was *A Guest of Honor* in that trunk?

Since 1950, The Case of the Missing Opera has engaged and baffled serious ragtime buffs. One comes up with a rumor: "X says Y told him that someone—maybe Z—just found the manuscript in a music store in St Louis." Next time around the music store was in Columbia, Missouri.

Then rumor has it that *A Guest of Honor* is in an ancient iron Wells Fargo safe in Nevada City, California. Then it is in one in Carson City, Nevada. Then a Sedalia informant claims to have found the first three pages of the original manuscript. Culled from these (but not seen by anyone else) comes a supposed list of numbers from the opera: *Sundown Rag, Jubilee Rag, Freedom's Etude, Elijah's Drag, Butler's Drag, Reception Rag, State Fair Rag,* etc. The scene of the opera, says the informant, was a reception in the Missouri Governor's mansion. And the guest of honor?

Scott Joplin himself. May anyone see these precious pages? No!

Well. . . .

All this, of course, is the lighter side of a most melancholy matter. The fate of *A Guest of Honor* is the sad tale of what might have been, for the time was right (and the public ready) for a syncopated American opera. *A Guest of Honor,* however, was not the first opera by a black-American composer. In 1893 *The Martyr* by Harry Lawrence Freeman (1870-1954) had been produced in Denver. Freeman subsequently composed more than a dozen operas, mostly based on American Negro, Indian, African, and Oriental subjects, many of which were widely performed under Freeman's direction. He wrote at least one jazz opera in the 1920s, and his work *Voodoo* is believed to be the first Negro opera on a Negro theme and performed by a Negro cast to have been produced on Broadway (1928). He and Joplin knew each other and Joplin's interest in composing operas may very well have been stimulated by his familiarity with some of Freeman's earlier works.[14]

In 1904 St Louis got its World's Fair after a year's postponement; John Stark & Son resumed the publication of Joplin rags; and the composer himself continued to develop and refine his syncopated piano pieces. Four rags were published: *The Cascades, The Sycamore, The Chrysanthemum,* and *The Favorite.*

Only *The Favorite* belongs melodically and structurally wholly to the Sedalia period and in fact was published there by A. W. Perry & Sons who in 1898 had turned down the *Maple Leaf Rag.* The ragtime player, composer, and Joplinophile, Trebor Jay Tichenor of St Louis, says

14 See Edward Ellsworth Hipscher *American Opera and Its Composers* (Philadelphia: Theodore Presser Co 1927) 189-195 and *Baker's Biographical Dictionary of Musicians,* 5th ed, completely revised by Nicolas Slonimsky (New York: G. Schirmer 1958) 509-510. In August 1971 Mr Valdo Freeman, the composer's son, provided his father's correct birth date and confirmed that his father and Joplin were friends.

that Perry had bought *The Favorite* in 1900. With *Maple Leaf* such a hit, one wonders why they delayed publication of *The Favorite* for four years.

The Cascades is program music with its subject the Cascade Gardens, the notable watercourse of fountains, lagoons, and cascades that was a central feature of the Fair. A virtuoso piece, it too flows and ripples while building an infectious swing. Though not indicated in the score, in performance this work seems naturally to tend towards a gradual acceleration. The treble part is customarily played an octave higher in the repeat, an effect that is often heard in ragtime playing, and actually indicated in the scores of both *The Entertainer* and *Elite Syncopations*. The correspondence of all this to Negro vocal practices should not be considered accidental. The singing in many black churches, then and now, builds tension through gradual speedup, while the women's voices often echo the preacher's phrases.

In the body of Joplin's work, *The Cascades* looks in both directions. The first theme has an ascending *arpeggio* similar to the one in the *Maple Leaf*, but this time in sixths. The fourth theme leans harmonically on *Maple Leaf* while the trio shows an interesting development in a "stride" bass that intermittently breaks into thundering octaves reminiscent of those characteristically shouted out by Sousa's trombones.

The Cascades clearly indicates its composer's ability, while continually refining his material, to retain undiminished the earthy vigor and native force of black folk-elements. While others were merely "ragging the classics"—syncopating war horses like Mendelssohn's *Spring Song* or his ubiquitous *Wedding March*—Joplin was effecting a basic, germinative fusion of disparate materials.

In the 1904 works there are interesting developments in many directions. *The Sycamore* features an increasingly free bass line with contrapuntal answers to the treble. *The Chrysanthemum* presents a teasing, whirling little pattern *à la bourrée*. *Chrysanthemum* is also the first

Joplin rag to use a trio of a particularly personal, caressing quality, gently syncopated and marked *piano* and *dolce*. This mood, though far from the wine-room world, still retains the quintessential swing.

Also published in 1904 was the *Maple Leaf Rag—Song*, the first of two such adaptations; the *Pine Apple Rag—Song* followed six years later. Both are highly superior to the other Joplin songs, excluding those in his longer works. They are gay, catchy, slangy, and extremely singable, making no bows to the often maudlin taste in songs of the period.

The excellence derives in no small part from their lyrics—lyric writing, certainly, was not among Joplin's outstanding gifts. Sydney Brown's adroitly rhymed words for the *Maple Leaf Song* contain such gems in the verse as the following:

> I dropped into de swellest ball
> The great exclusive 'IT',
> But my face was dead agin me
> And my trousers didn't fit;
>
> But when Maple Leaf was started
> My timidity departed,
> I lost my trepidation.
> You could taste de admiration.

In the chorus the words rise to a kind of ragtime triumph.

The tangy vernacular prosody fits rhythm and melody like the proverbial glove. They are worthy of the famous music. Joplin's fascination with the dance continues here: two of the original themes are sung, but trio and fourth theme are for solo piano and entitled: *DANCE—Either or both strains may be used for the dance.*

ON THE MOVE

The year 1905 brought the publication of five works. Only one is a piano rag: *Leola—Two Step*, which was first registered at Stationer's Hall, London. One of the rarest of the Joplin rags, it was not really known until the 1950s when Dr Hubert S. Pruett of St Louis found a copy. *Leola* has a first subject punctuated by octaves for both hands and a second strain of flowing melody employing thirds in the manner then known as the "Spanish" or "La Paloma" style.

Joplin habitually gave his rags tempo designations like *Tempo di marcia*, "Slow march tempo," or simply "Not fast." With *Leola* he began adding the warning that would be seen in most of his works to come:

> Notice! Don't play this piece fast. It is never right to play "rag-time" fast. Author.

With the ragtime revival of the 1940s, some younger players interpreted these instructions over-literally, slowing some inherently lively pieces down to a dispirited walk. In extreme cases *Tempo di marcia* almost became *Marche funèbre*. The newcomers felt that, though it might not swing, ragtime was being played in the authentic manner. Actually, any piece of music dictates—within rather clear limits—its own proper tempo. Joplin's injunction needs to be read in the light of his time, when a whole school of "speed" players whose sole claim to fame was digital velocity were ruining the fine rags. Most frequently felled by this quack-virtuoso musical mayhem was the *Maple Leaf*. Joplin's concept of "slow" was probably relative to the destructive *prestos* of his day.

In 1905, *The Rosebud March* appeared, dedicated to Tom Turpin, and named for the famous saloon. It is a rousing 6/8 piece with a thirty-two bar trio that is both songlike and waltzlike.

There were two waltzes in 1905, each charming and one of them important in the composer's development. *Binks' Waltz* is a tuneful, well-written three-theme piece with instructions for tempo, dynamics, and *rubato*. The other waltz, *Bethena*, is perhaps Joplin's finest waltz. It clearly earns its subtitle of "concert waltz" but, unlike *Binks'*, *Bethena* is a ragtime waltz, a fully syncopated piece in 3/4 time. Syncopation, which in 2/4 ragtime is a thing of great excitement, in 3/4 becomes a subtler intoxicant. *Bethena's* five

smooth and elegant themes, in five different tonalities, are connected by deft transitional passages. The introduction and coda are built on the same fragment of the first theme.

In 1905 one Joplin song was published, *Sarah Dear*, with words again by Henry Jackson. Although the chorus of *Sarah Dear* is identical with the then current Barney-Seymour hit rag, *The St. Louis Tickle*, none of the composers involved had priority, for the tune was a ribald song of the Mississippi riverboat roustabouts. It had appeared six years before in Ben Harney's *Cakewalk In the Sky* and during the same period in New Orleans. Jelly Roll Morton recalled it as the theme song of the jazz pioneer, trumpeter Charles "Buddy" Bolden, with lyrics only slightly sanitized from the levee camp versions:

> I thought I heard Buddy Bolden say
> "Nasty butt, stinky butt, take it away,
> Funky butt, stinky butt, take it away—"
> I thought I heard him say.

with Bolden's admonition to his tough little band to play "slow drag" and:

> 'Way down, 'way down low,
> So I can hear those whores
> Drag their feet across the floor!

Ill-fated Louis Chauvin used the same little melody in his 1906 song *Babe It's Too Long Off*. These folk ditties traveled far and wide, as sundry accounts show. Virgil Thomson recalls this same "funky butt" song on the Missouri River in his Kansas City boyhood, while Dr Newman Ivey White reported it as a work song in Augusta, Georgia, and a street song in Statesville, North Carolina.[15]

Jackson simply put words to a current folk ditty and Joplin wrote a piano accompaniment, though the music of the verse seems to be original. The chorus of *Sarah Dear* is his only known published use of an actual folk tune.

In 1905 tensions began to develop in the Joplin

15 Newman I. White *American Negro Folk-Songs* (Cambridge: Harvard University Press 1928) 279.

household. A baby girl had been born but, ill from birth, she survived only a few months. The boarding house residents knew little of the domestic troubles brewing but Arthur Marshall remembered that Joplin's "composing and teaching of ragtime music was greatly disturbed." Marshall was tactful and delicate in detailing this critical phase in the life of his friend, father-figure, and benefactor:

> Mrs. Joplin wasn't so interested in music and her taking violin lessons from Scott was a perfect failure. Mr. Joplin was seriously humiliated. Of course unpleasant attitudes and lack of home interests occurred between them.
> They finally separated. He told me his wife had no interest in his music career. Otherwise Mrs. Joplin was very pleasant to his friends and especially to we home boys. But the other side was strictly theirs. To other acquaintances of the family other than I and Hayden and also my brother Lee who knew the facts, Scott was towards her in their presence very pleasing.
> A shield of honor toward her existed and for the child. As my brother . . . Hayden and I were like his brothers, Joplin often asked us to console Mrs. Joplin—perhaps she would reconsider. But she remained neutral. She never was harsh with us, but we just couldn't get her to see the point. So a separation finally resulted. (*TAPR* 79-80)

It was early in 1906 that the Joplins parted. He went to Chicago and for a short while stayed with the Marshalls, Arthur having married and moved to Chicago in the interim.

> He went . . . to see some publishers. He said they received him cordially. Perhaps they didn't talk to suit him, so he never said more. . . . He was very eager to go to New York. This was the last time that I ever saw him. (*TAPR* 231)

It is likely that Joplin had little new music to offer for publication and was only making contacts, for in the year 1906 only two publications appeared, both issued by Stark. One is a condensed piano version of *The Ragtime Dance*, known from Stark family reports to have been an attempt to recoup the losses on the longer version. The other is the 6/8 march, *Antoinette,*

which, on stylistic evidence, may have been written a year or two earlier.

Joplin did not move east directly from Chicago, though the Stark head office was already in New York on Twenty-third Street, just east of the new but already famous Flatiron Building. He was restless and uncertain. Toward the end of the year he went back to St Louis and until well into 1907 lived with the Tom Turpins, working on new rags. That same year he also visited Texarkana before he finally moved on to New York and a new life.

Before this, however, during the difficult year of 1906 and while still in Chicago, Joplin managed to collaborate on one memorable rag with the fading Louis Chauvin, trapped in the Chicago red-light district and lacking the will to leave. When Joplin went to see him, it was all too obvious that the still romantically handsome youth of twenty-four was nearing his end. The gifted Creole—part Ibo, part Indian, and part French—was smoking opium and beginning to show the frightful terminal symptoms of syphilis. In less than eighteen months after Joplin's visit he was dead.

Yet in that disordered, penultimate time, Chauvin was still fitfully creating ragtime. He had two beautiful themes at hand and right there in the bawdy-house parlor, as Sam Patterson has related, Joplin sketched two of his own.[16] The fruit of the visit is thirty-two measures of music saved from the unpublished prodigality of a heedless, wastrel genius. They are the first two themes of one of the masterpieces of ragtime literature, the Joplin-Chauvin *Heliotrope Bouquet,* issued by Stark in 1907.

Conforming with Joplin's propensity for floral, folial, and arboreal titles, *Heliotrope Bouquet* validates its name by the atmosphere of Chauvin's themes, clothed in his exquisitely personal harmony. They are as darkly perfumed as a Chopin nocturne. Joplin's trio and fourth subject are at once a comment on the Chauvin themes and a

16 Conversation with Rudi Blesh and Harriet Janis, New York, November 1949.

farewell to a friend. Evidently moved both by the music and his personal knowledge of the Chauvin story, John Stark advertised *Heliotrope* as "the audible poetry of motion."

The publication marks the end of the year, with Joplin already based in New York. The year as a whole had witnessed large publication: no less than eight issues, including two songs, two collaborative rags and four by Joplin alone. Three of the four quietly announce a profound maturing taking place.

The songs are *Snoring Sampson,* with words by Harry La Mertha, and *When Your Hair Is Like the Snow,* to lyrics by Owen Spendthrift. No copy of the former could be located but, on the evidence of its title and the ascertainable quality of the latter, both can be dismissed without further comment as potboilers.

Heliotrope Bouquet, of course, is one of the 1907 collaborative pieces; the other, *Lily Queen,* is a ragtime two-step co-composed with Marshall. Hiding behind its cover artwork—a charming pompadoured Gibson Girl niched in lilies—the *Lily Queen* expresses two musical personalities: Marshall and early Missouri, and Joplin, searcher for wider horizons. On musical evidence, Marshall's themes come first, the A strain a nicely chorded march, followed by a flowing second theme. With the trio we move into the new—a ragtime infinitely more sophisticated yet pensive as well, with portents of the muted melancholy of Joplin rags that were to come. A chromatic descending figure from Chauvin's second *Heliotrope* theme is quoted in the trio and the final lyrical strain makes striking use of recurrent *appoggiaturas.*

Of the four 1907 rags by Joplin alone, only *Nonpareil* (published by Stark) looks back in the main to the Sedalia-St Louis years. The others are of a different time and place, a musical remove as wide and decisive as their composer's physical move to New York. With the rags *Searchlight, Gladiolus,* and *Rose Leaf* we find a creative flow that is melodic but also deeper, richer, more reflective, and more assured.

Perhaps the many decisive changes in Joplin's personal life—the death of his infant daughter and (shortly after their separation) of his wife, his move to New York after restless wandering—may have contributed to the expanded direction his creative work was now following.

Searchlight Rag was published by Joseph W. Stern of New York. The title is an implied compliment to Tom Turpin and his brother Charlie, a reference to the town of Searchlight, Nevada, where, about 1881, the brothers had been seeking gold in the Big Onion Mine. *Searchlight Rag* abounds in elements that show Joplin's loyalty to his American past as well as his ability to transmute these vernacular source materials into exquisitely wrought compositions. In the second theme, for example, the ragtime stride bass alternates with the "barrel house" walking bass in octaves, and in the fourth theme there occur the jangly, pleasantly dissonant treble chords then called "crazy chords."

Gladiolus Rag is one of the most successful of all Joplin rags in its realization of the special nature of rag form. This, in effect, began as non-form, a simple sequence of four tunes. Joplin saw more in it; saw, too, that were the rag, on its own terms, to become more than a loose necklace of tunes, the themes must in some way build, that is, form a meaningful sequence.

The problem was made difficult by the special characteristics of the rag: uniform tempo and a single meter throughout. There also was avoidance of thematic development: a theme, stated and reprised, was always the same.

Granted that many of these quirks had arisen from musical semi-literacy: still, to have invoked more elaborate technical procedures would in the end have all but completely transformed its basic flavor. Whatever his reason, Joplin chose the harder course: that of creating meaningful music without changing the rag's own rules.

His first composed (although second published) ragtime essay, the *Maple Leaf Rag,* indicated the direction his solution would take: the opening theme must capture ear and imagination; then each succeeding theme must form an episode in a musical story. Ideally, then, the final theme should say the last word or else invite a restatement of the first words.

Almost to perfection, *Gladiolus Rag* realizes this narrative quality of cumulative emotion and developing musical thought. Its final theme is so definitely a strong concluding statement that a reentry of any of the earlier themes is almost inconceivable.

Rose Leaf Rag, published by Joseph Daly of Boston, is another 1907 masterpiece. Like *Searchlight Rag* and the 1908 *Fig Leaf Rag,* it unavoidably had to be omitted from this edition. (See Editor's Note, p xi above.) With *Searchlight, Gladiolus,* and *Rose Leaf,* the development of the new musical genus, the classic rag, becomes clearly evident. Here is an American composer cultivating and developing an American music—not in the doff-the-hat-to-Europe way of many American composers of his day, but in terms of the scope and needs of the material itself—and with justice to its dual origins: Black Africa, White America. As cultural anthropologist von Hornbostel long ago observed, ragtime is a new music in cultural history.[17]

Scott Joplin was a slow, painstaking composer. The long list of his 1907 publications is remarkable in view of the busy public life he was leading. Determining upon more varied activity, and feeling that his classic ragtime needed his personal missionary work, he embarked upon a series of vaudeville tours, carrying on his composition in boarding houses and hotels en route. He toured intermittently, billed as "King of Ragtime Composers—Author of *Maple Leaf Rag.*"

LIFE IN NEW YORK

But the nomadic life was no longer for Scott Joplin. Nor, indeed—for a man whose capacity for love is so clearly avowed in his music—was the single life. In New York he met Lottie Stokes and in 1909 they were married. She accompanied him as he wound down his public, touring life and then, back in New York, they set up the kind of theatrical boarding-house-cum-conservatory that seemed his natural habitat. Their first house was at 252 West Forty-seventh Street. Sam Patterson and others remembered this house and the later one uptown. Joplin devoted himself to music-teaching and the careful, seemingly endless work on manuscripts, one, in particular now, that already bore a title: *Treemonisha, Opera in Three Acts.* Mrs Joplin saw to the housekeeping, shopping, cooking and serving of meals, and the more or less lenient collecting of bills.

The rags that Scott Joplin now wrote are clearly pages of an autobiography without words. Few passages of his earlier works contain such tenderly intimate revelations as those in *Wall Street Rag* —especially the trio—or the ardor of his Mexican tango-serenade *Solace.* Lottie Stokes, after all his losses, must have been solace and more. At least, this is what the music seems to say, and of all possible explanations it might best explain the unleashing of creative powers that came with with marriage.

Joplin was a natural teacher, too. A fruit of his teaching activity is his ragtime instruction manual, *The School of Ragtime,* which he himself published in 1908. It contains six piano exercises and was modestly priced at fifty cents a copy. It was not the first instruction book in piano syncopation. As early as 1897 Ben Harney had issued his *Rag Time Instructor.* And, after *Maple Leaf Rag* became the technical frustration of thousands of amateur pianists, teachers began opening studios and hanging out the signs: "Learn to play ragtime and be popular." The "come-on," of course, was the famous slogan: "They laughed when I sat down at the piano." Many schools opened, and many manuals appeared. Most successful of the new entrepreneurs was Axel Christensen whose schools became a chain that operated in twenty-five cities, including Honolulu.

[17] Erich von Hornbostel "African Negro Music" in *Africa* vol I, no 1 (London: The African Society, n. d.) .

The courses that led to the "diplomas" in rag-time were a cursory "Ragtime in Ten Easy Lessons" that helped to stereotype the music as a frivolous popular fad. Scott Joplin's pedagogy was serious in approach, as well as disdainful of the popular slogans and misconceptions. He bluntly prefaced his exercises:

That real ragtime of the higher class is rather difficult to play is a painful truth which most pianists have discovered. Syncopations are no indication of light or trashy music, and to shy bricks at "hateful ragtime" no longer passes for musical culture.

Three piano rags were completed by Joplin and published in the same year as the *School of Ragtime*. These are *Fig Leaf, Sugar Cane,* and *Pine Apple Rag. Fig Leaf* is a somewhat ambivalent piece. The first two themes are in an earlier Joplin style. With the trio, the harmony darkens into richer chords, and the scene shifts from pastoral to theatrical. The trio is almost visually choreographic, and the last theme comes on like an opera chorus singing and marching.

Sugar Cane is equally—but differently—diversified in content: a first theme intentionally "classic"; a second theme contrastingly "popular"; a whirling, tango-tinged trio as *art nouveau* and seductive as the curvesome sylphs of the Mucha posters.

Individuality is maintained in the *Pine Apple Rag,* with its narrative, almost balladic structure. The story begins, lively but innocent. The second section begins to sway with Joplinesque between-the-beat phrasing; then it is the A theme back like a return to innocence. Suddenly the music plunges into an American red-light bacchanale—dark, chromatic, fully-chorded, *forte* and "low down." The dance surges on into the D theme, stomping above a moving, contrapuntal bass line.

Joplin had launched the careers of two composers, Marshall and Hayden; he now did the same for a young white aspirant who went on to become one of ragtime's finest composers, black or white. It was late in 1907 or early the following year that Joseph Francis Lamb dropped into the Stark & Son store. As a steady customer for ragtime sheet music, he was allowed a cash discount. This visit, however, developed into something more momentous. The memories were still vivid as he told about it in 1949:

There was a colored fellow sitting there with his foot bandaged up as if he had the gout, and a crutch beside him. I hardly noticed him. I told Mrs. Stark that I liked the Joplin rags best and wanted to get any I didn't have. The colored fellow spoke up and asked whether I had certain pieces which he named. I thanked him and bought several and was leaving when I said to Mrs. Stark that Joplin was one fellow I would certainly like to meet.

"Really," said Mrs. Stark. "Well, here's your man." I shook hands with him, needless to say. It was a thrill I've never forgotten. I had met Scott Joplin and was going home to tell the folks.

Mrs. Stark told him I had sent in a couple of rags for their approval. I had, all right, and they had come back two days later. Joplin seemed interested and asked if he could walk up the street with me. We walked along Twenty-third Street and into Madison Square Park and sat on a bench.

Mr. Joplin asked if my rags were really good. I said, "To me they seem all right—maybe they are not. I don't know." He invited me to bring them over to his place. Needless to say, I didn't waste time.

I went to his boarding house a few evenings later and he asked me to play my pieces on the piano in the parlor. A lot of colored people were sitting around talking. I played my *Sensation* first and they began to crowd around and watch me. When I finished, Joplin said, "That's a good rag—a regular Negro rag." That's what I wanted to hear. . . . Joplin liked *Sensation* best of my first three rags. (*TAPR* 236)

At this first hearing Joplin offered to present *Sensation* to Stark personally. Lamb recalled that Joplin said: "We will put on along with your name: 'arranged by Scott Joplin.' People do not know you and my name might help sell the rag." Joplin was as good as his word. "He wanted to get me going," Lamb said. "A week later a letter came from Stark offering me twenty-five dollars and an equal sum after the first printing of one thousand was sold. He could have had it for nothing—I wanted to see it published. I got the other twenty-five dollars in a month. Then he bought *Ethiopia* and *Excelsior* together. After that he took any rag I wrote" (*TAPR* 237).

The extent to which classic ragtime was published—despite the flood of Tin-Pan Alley's cheap imitations—is due in great measure to Joplin's generosity and vision. James Scott and Joseph Lamb, two men he assisted, are ragtime composers of the first rank, and the work of Marshall and Hayden as well as Chauvin's only published rag survive mainly because of him.

With these men in the vanguard, a music of black origin became a music for all, a young tradition with the resources to move from short piano pieces to larger forms. Composer might follow composer, each working with individuality while carrying a unified tradition forward. What ragtime needed now was to receive some modicum of sanction from the "serious" music establishment.

The first decade-and-a-half of the century was the critical time for the new art. There was controversy enough. The merits of the ragtime case were lost in the noise. Despite the praise of eminent composers like Debussy and Dvořák, ragtime at home was, in the main, either pointedly ignored or actively attacked.

But in 1909, when Scott Joplin was forty-one years old, he was hopeful and determined, inspired and full of energy; and he can hardly have been at all cognizant of the crumbling precariousness, not only of his own career, but of the music he championed, symbolized, and so passionately believed in. It was a year notable in his life, both for the quantity, quality, and diversity of the work he wrote and saw published, and for the fact that he was fully launched on the opera, *Treemonisha*. After years of struggle he was at last in a position where creative work could be foremost.

The 1909 rags include *Wall Street, Country Club, Euphonic Sounds,* and *Paragon.* There is also a waltz, *Pleasant Moments,* and the Mexican serenade, *Solace.* Taken together—without the work on an opera—these six pieces would constitute a notable year. The entire year's output, like several works of the year before, was published by Seminary Music Company.

By this time John Stark was running into difficulties. His wife had become ill and had returned to St Louis to be cared for by relatives. The Eastern venture—in fact, classic ragtime itself—was not faring well. Neither the Missouri pioneer nor his catalogue fitted into the Tin-Pan Alley scheme of things. And Tin-Pan Alley now dominated the popular field. Stark's country-peddler shrewdness was somewhat hobbled by his missionary zeal for the music he had chosen to champion, as well as by a personal honesty that drew a distinct line between the shrewd and the sharp. Neither ruthlessness nor compromise was a part of his strong nature. His generation had believed that trade thrived on fair competition; it gave a place to the little business man.

Stark fought back as best he could, but he was losing. A cruel price war, utilizing five-and-ten-cent-store counters, was driving out the small independent publishers and the music business was consolidating. Soon after Sarah Ann Stark died in 1910, he wrote off the Eastern venture and returned to St Louis.

TREEMONISHA & THE LAST PIANO PIECES

Joplin meanwhile continued to work on his opera. He seemed to be thinking mostly in terms of larger forms. In the seven years he had left to live, only five more Joplin rags would be published, two of these of seemingly earlier composition.

With this new direction, matters of training and his own conceptual equipment became paramount. He clearly had become the foremost master of the classic rag's short form. Developing this, he had attempted to supplement his spotty early training by intensive study on his own. In 1904, while still in St Louis, he had bought a copy of the new edition of Jadassohn's 1891 book: *A Manual of Simple, Double, Triple and Quadruple Coun-*

terpoint. That it was thoroughly used is evident not only from its well-thumbed and marginally-noted condition but also by the contrapuntal devices that then began to enter into his music.

The successful long form, however—whether symphony, concerto, oratorio, or opera—is not only a matter for special study but one of a special bent of mind. *Treemonisha*'s overture and three acts would test Joplin's training and his natural aptitude.

Nothing in his earlier training had prepared Joplin for working in extended forms. The whole world he grew up in lacked continuities and meaningful interrelationships: the kaleidoscopic shuttle of the town-to-town itinerant in raw new settlements, the night world of the red lights, the hokum vaudeville that had evolved from blackface minstrelsy. He had had the will and vision to flee it all, but his formative years had been lived there. That even such a mastery of short form and patient striving for perfection could have survived this charivari is a miracle.

No matter: in this year of his dedication to writing an opera, the six short piano pieces he published would assure him of a high place in American music, were these all that Joplin had ever written.

Solace—A Mexican Serenade is his only work in tango rhythm. Originally from Cuba, by way of the African cult houses where it is said to have been known by its African tribal name, *tangana*, this rhythm had entered American piano literature as early as 1860 with Louis Moreau Gottschalk's *Souvenir de la Havane*. The first reported instance of tango in the unchronicled history of American Negro music is a rag-tango called *The Dream*, composed and played by an itinerant black player, Jess Pickett, at the Chicago World's Fair in 1893. A famous Afro-American tango, Will H. Tyer's *Maori*, was published in 1908 just a year before the Joplin piece. *Solace*, however, does not resemble *Maori*; it is pure Joplin from beginning to end and a superb work. *Pleasant Moments*, like the earlier *Bethena*, is a syncopated waltz, equally pure in style but less brilliant and more tender.

Wall Street Rag, within its territory of mood, is one of the most perfectly realized of all Joplin rags. One is misled by the title "Wall Street" and by the descriptive headings over the themes: "Panic in Wall Street, Brokers feeling melancholy"; "Good times coming"; "Good times have come"; "Listening to the strains of genuine negro ragtime, brokers forget their cares." Dismiss all this trumpery and whatever aberration invoked it in this tender piece—there is nothing here to do with Mammon: never was a piece of music so mistitled. *Wall Street Rag* is another little ballade in rag form, romantic and essentially aristocratic.

Country Club Rag is a study in alternate ideas: ballet and song. The A theme is dancelike; B is a singing refrain. Trio is dance again, and the final strain, song. This mixture of song and dance elements encourages the belief that, with the access to staged performances that he never fully achieved, Scott Joplin might have been an effective composer for choreography.

Even in those days, it was chiefly on the light opera stage that experimental couplings of choreography and song could be ventured. It seems likely that Joplin might have made a lasting contribution there, not only because of his melodic gifts and love of the dance, but also because of his fidelity to his own race and its folklore. While Bert Williams was declaring that "the colored performer would have to get away from the ragtime limitations of the 'darky,' "[18] Joplin was creating classic ragtime out of the rich earthy beauties of the black music of church and dance hall. Had he, perhaps, not placed his faith in a foredoomed opera and had chosen, instead, to work in musical comedy he might have wrought early changes, bringing to the theatre folk essences that had to wait many years: for a *Porgy and Bess*, an *Oklahoma!*, a *Dark of the Moon*, a *Voodoo*.

The great variety of the 1909 rags is maintained by *Euphonic Sounds*. Modestly subtitled "A Syncopated Two Step," *Euphonic Sounds* is far from modest in intent or realization. Here, once and

18 See *The Theatre* (August 1906) 224 et seq.

for all, Joplin shows how to free the piano rag of the perpetual "oompah" bass. There are not a half-dozen measures of stride bass in the entire piece. The swinging polyrhythms are achieved by other figurations.

Euphonic Sounds moves all the way into rondo form, being thematically arranged: A-B-A-C-A with repeats. A difficult piece to play, it became a noted challenge to the eastern ragtime school of "shout" pianists. Lonnie Hicks of Philadelphia and the "shout" master, James P. Johnson, were famed for their ease in performing its intricacies. In 1944, thirty-five years after its publication, Johnson recorded it, playing with undaunted virtuosity even while—in the delightful, incorrigible eastern way—adding "shout" embellishments of his own. A few years later, reminiscing, he said, "Joplin was a great forerunner. He was fifty years ahead of his time. Even today, who understands *Euphonic Sounds*? It's really modern" (*TAPR* 204).

Continuing the 1909 emphasis on variety, *Paragon Rag* has the plantation sound, its first theme almost a buck-and-wing. The second theme is interesting on two counts. First, the melody is the same as the traditional New Orleans bawdy-house song, *Bucket's Got a Hole in It—Can't Get No Beer,* but whether the song came from the rag or if, much earlier, Joplin heard it while on his youthful travels, is anybody's guess. Second, this strain introduces right-hand "breaks" that immediately became a trademark of the "player-piano" style of roll-recording players like Pete Wendling. Ragtime roll collector Michael Montgomery also notes that these break figures were used by Zez Confrey in his late-period 1921 rag, *Kitten On the Keys.* Plantation sounds continue into *Paragon's* trio with its banjoesque "single-string" treble over a chorded bass.

In 1910, with the composer concentrating almost totally on *Treemonisha,* there were only two publications. One, *Pine Apple Rag—Song,* as previously noted, was a 1908 piano rag set to words. The other, *Stoptime Rag,* is a rhythmic delight capturing, as no other Joplin rag, the salty prodi-

gies of nineteenth-century American folk dance—frontier, minstrel, and Afro-American.

The term "stoptime" refers to tacets, that is, to "stopping the time" in the accompaniment, whether banjos, rustic fiddle, or ragtime piano. Dancer or dancers filled the tacets with the sounds of feet on the floor, similarly accenting some of the sounded beats. The foot sounds might be those of sliding feet, especially on sand sprinkled on the boards (as in the Virginia Essence). The "slow drag" was a variation of the "slide." Foot-stampings—called "stomps"—came in around the turn of the century, and more or less at the same time came the virtuosities of tap-dancing.

It is worthy of notice that, in the midst of composing an opera, Joplin could write a little whirlwind *scherzo* like *Stoptime Rag.* To it he brought a special zest, and a freedom from some of the strictions of the piano rag form that he himself had had so considerable a hand in developing. Here (and here only) is found the amazing (for Joplin) tempo direction: "Fast or slow," with music written to be adapted to any tempo—as if the dancer, not he, were calling the tune and setting the time. Both versions of *The Ragtime Dance* include a stoptime section with the same *"Stamp"* instructions that appear in *Stoptime Rag. Stoptime Rag* whirls with a scintillating gaiety that provides the rare moment in which the grave black man, of whom John Stark observed that "he was never caught smiling," not only smiled but laughed out loud.

Following *Stoptime Rag* no new Joplin piano rag would appear for a year and a half and then it would be a collaborative piece with Hayden. The first two themes of *Felicity Rag* are almost surely by Hayden and might be from 1907 or earlier. The trio seems Joplinesque and stylistically post-1908. Perhaps Joplin had brought along an incomplete Hayden manuscript when he moved to New York, later adding the completing trio. The final Joplin-Hayden rag *Kismet Rag,* issued in 1913, tends to strengthen this theory. *Kismet* is also a three-theme rag although it ends with a variant of the A theme figuration.

Only two more Joplin rags were to be published during the composer's lifetime. These are *Scott Joplin's New Rag* issued by Stern in 1912, and *Magnetic Rag* published by Joplin himself in 1914. *Reflection Rag* was brought out by Stark late in 1917, eight months after Joplin's death.

His last years were almost totally devoted to his opera: its composition, its publication, orchestration, and trial performance, and his continual, futile attempts to get it produced. There were rumors toward the end of his life that Joplin was working on a ragtime symphony. This seems doubtful in view of his utter obsession with *Treemonisha,* coupled with his declining health. No trace of sketches for such a work were found among his musical effects in 1949-50 when Joplin's widow was being interviewed in connection with the writing of the history, *They All Played Ragtime.*

Scott Joplin's New Rag is as joyous and triumphant in its way as the *Maple Leaf.* It is the last rag in this vein that Joplin would ever complete. *Magnetic Rag* fully justifies its unusual subtitle: *Syncopations classiques.* It covers a range of moods unusual even in Joplin's work, one that almost strains the capacity of the short form. *Magnetic* as pure music is an impressive, although sadly premature, close to Scott Joplin's piano works. It hints at future directions and demonstrates ragtime's potential capability of expressing profounder musical thought.

Magnetic Rag was published in July 1914. To return to 1911: Scott Joplin's collaborative piece with Hayden, *Felicity Rag,* was published by Stark. In the broader sense of the fate of ragtime as a whole, the year 1911 witnessed the resounding popular success of young Irving Berlin's rag-song, *Alexander's Ragtime Band.* Classic piano ragtime was waning as Tin-Pan Alley took over with pseudo-rags and rag-songs. The real rag classics, originally championed by Stark, were supplanted by more easily played and more salable items, brought out by an enlarged music industry that had developed wider sales outlets.

Songs, though never the forte of a Scott Joplin or a James Scott, were the popular staple, anyway. Practically anyone could hum, whistle, or even yodel a *Hello Ma Baby,* but the *Euphonic Sounds* resisted such sidewalk embraces. Black-music historian Eileen Southern contrasts the "captivating but rather vapid style of the ragtime song [with] the essence of serious rag music," and observes that by "1910 the rag professors were either writing fewer and fewer rags or were moving over into other areas of musical activity." The publication of the Berlin song, she adds, "was in reality the swan song of the ragtime-song period, although it brought about a brief revival of interest in the music."[19]

Far more importantly: in May of 1911 the complete score of *Treemonisha,* refused by music publishers to whom it had been submitted, was brought out at the composer's own expense and with his own imprint. This Afro-American folk opera is an ambitious score for eleven voices and choruses with piano accompaniment. Although it may not be a grand opera in the conventional sense, *Treemonisha,* with all its libretto shortcomings, is a glorious compendium of beautiful Afro-American music, authentic and pure. The opera contains twenty-seven set pieces (though several are short transitions) and includes an overture to Act One, an introductory passage to Act Two, and a prelude to Act Three. Though the story has continuity, the musical numbers are separate: each is complete and separately titled and numbered in the score.

The story is a black folk fable with the intent of parable. The music, correspondingly, is largely more faithful to the folk idiom than the piano rags, where similar material is treated with greater sophistication. For reasons of this fidelity to source (which must have been a compelling motivation) *Treemonisha* (book and score alike) is both naive and sophisticated, innocent and philosophical, trite in spots and yet gripping. It is the work of a genius, whatever its naïvete.

19 Eileen Southern *The Music of Black Americans: A History* (New York: W. W. Norton & Co 1971) 330.

As to the book: if not so accomplished a writer as Joel Chandler Harris, Scott Joplin was a real, not surrogate, spokesman for his race, as Harris or his semi-fictional Uncle Remus could never be. Nothing in all the Remus animal fabulism is as eerie or strange as the surrealist scene of Joplin's mountain bears waltzing in the forest.

How Treemonisha was found as a baby (under a tree), adopted, and given an education, is told by Joplin in his Preface to the opera. The rest of her story: how she fought the black conjurors and their Voodoo magic, and how she escaped their plot to kill her, became the leader of her people (Women's Liberation papers, please copy), and began to lead them to freedom and equality through education—all of this is the story told in the opera itself. But it is more: its subject (then and now) is Black America and its creator was capable of outlining (with an opera as his vehicle) an early program for black action.

Treemonisha is truly Scott Joplin's last testament as an artist and a black American. The music heard during his early years of wandering, and long since taken root in his memory, now flowers into a true racial expression. Its rich color is here: in a corn-huskers' ring dance, in moving choral responses and in the uncanny blue "moaning" behind closed lips in the "Superstition" scene of Act Two. Then the music may veer affectionately into the timeless Americanese of barber-shop harmony, or Aunt Dinah may blow the horn in a real "quittin' time song" as the sun sets and the laborers come in from the fields.

And, to ring down the curtain, there is the hauntingly melodious ragtime finale, *A Real Slow Drag,* with its prancing and triumphant conclusion.

Joplin called *A Guest of Honor* a ragtime opera; *Treemonisha,* he did not. Clearly, in the later work he aimed to combine ragtime and folk music with more conventional musical expression. *Treemonisha* aims to go beyond the rag form to bring ragtime (or its essence) into the musical mainstream.

Publishing the *Treemonisha* score was a heavy drain on Joplin's funds. Nevertheless, without delay he set about orchestrating the work and getting the instrumental parts written out, while at the same time attempting to get backing for a production. However unrealistic, his hopes ran high.

THE FINAL YEARS

But Joplin was beginning to experience personal difficulties. Once so even in temperament, he was evincing extreme changes of mood. Unaccountably he would sink into brief, dark depressions which alternated with periods when his energy and concentration were phenomenal. Then he would work, almost without rest, on the opera instrumentation. To help finance his activity he took on more pupils.

In 1913, as New York Negroes migrated uptown, the Joplins moved to Harlem, buying a house at 163 West 131st Street. By that time *Treemonisha* had become Joplin's monomania. Even before it had been orchestrated and produced, he had apparently planned to publish its musical numbers separately. Drawing on already strained resources he brought out revised versions of *A Real Slow Drag,* and the *Prelude to Act 3* in 1913, and *Frolic of the Bears* in 1915.

Sam Patterson, one of the younger St Louis ragtimers and a friend of the ill-starred Chauvin, was now living in New York, and he was asked to help in preparing the orchestration. The following account was based on his memories:

He and Joplin would work all day in the basement apartment of the 131st Street house, Sam copying parts from the pages of the orchestral master score as Joplin finished them. At noon Lottie would bring their lunch in to them.

Sam describes a typical lunch: "Joplin said, 'Let's knock off, I hear Lottie coming.' Just then the phone rang and I went to answer it. When I came back there were fried eggs on the table and Lottie was opening a bottle of champagne some folks she worked for had given her. I said, 'These eggs are cold,' and Scott said, 'Look, Sam, if they're good hot, they're good cold.'" (*TAPR* 248-49)

Now unable to think of anything but the opera, Joplin began to neglect his pupils. Some left; he dismissed the others. Lottie was loyal. The financial situation worsened, then became desperate. Faced with emergency, she took decisive action: she prepared some rooms and took in "transient" guests. The house where Joplin was laboring on his opera is reported to have become a house of assignation.

With the orchestration of the opera under way, Joplin redoubled his efforts to attract backers. The downtown money was not interested: the concept of an opera by a black ragtime composer was just too much. In the hope of finding backing, he prepared a well-rehearsed audition for which he played the piano. Thus, finally, there was a single "performance" in 1915 in a hall in Harlem.

Joplin was a perfectionist. Patterson told how "he worked like a dog" rehearsing the cast. But he could not pre-condition his audience. It was a disastrous flop:

> Without scenery, costumes, lighting, or orchestral backing the drama seemed thin and unconvincing, little better than a rehearsal, and its special quality, in any event, would surely have been lost on the typical Harlem audience that attended. . . . sophisticated enough to reject their folk past but not sufficiently so to relish a return to it in art. (*TAPR* 249)

Joplin was crushed. As part of his obsession he had evidently placed all his hope in this one essentially desperate venture. He went back to work but the spark was gone. He began compositions but did not finish them. He began orchestrating his rags, to what end is not known. Among his effects, as seen in 1949-50 (and lost since the death of Mrs Joplin), were undated and incomplete orchestrations of *Stoptime Rag* and *Searchlight Rag* as well as two unfinished piano pieces, *Pretty Pansy Rag* and *Recitative Rag*. There was a partially completed song conversion of *Magnetic Rag*. There were incomplete songs, among them *For the Sake of All* and *Morning Glory,* and other items, some of them incoherent, unidentifiable scraps. Fragments of a fragmented life, they be-tokened a mind able to work only in sad, disoriented fits and starts.

The disorganization grew; the periods of deep depression lengthened as the lucid periods shrank; the physical coordination began failing, then worsened at an accelerated speed.

A player-piano roll made by Joplin is frightening evidence of the composer's rapid disintegration. Joplin's playing had not been recorded on rolls until the year before he died. In April 1916 he played several rolls for the Connorized label. Among these was a smooth, competent version of *Maple Leaf Rag*. In June, only ten months before his death, Joplin recorded the *Maple Leaf* again, this time for the Uni-record Melody player-roll label. The change that had taken place in two months is shocking. The second version is disorganized and completely distressing to hear. Early that fall Mrs Joplin at last was forced to have him committed.

> [He] was removed to the Manhattan State Hospital on Ward's Island in the East River along the strait called Hell Gate. Lottie relates that even at the hospital there were moments when the composer began once more feverishly jotting notes on bits of paper. But the flashes were dimmer and dimmer, and at length all was dark. On April 1, 1917, Scott Joplin died. (*TAPR* 249)

In 1950 the widow still regretted that she had refused the request her husband had so often made for the *Maple Leaf Rag* to be played at his funeral.

The Tenderloin, which had given young Scott Joplin his first chance in a nearly closed society, gave him his early death. The cause, as stated by his death certificate: "Dementia Paralytica-cerebral," and the contributing cause: "Syphilis."

The abrupt and untimely cutting off of creative genius constitutes a tragedy which affects us all. It is so with Scott Joplin, who had contributed, during the mere twenty years or so of his creativity, a unique legacy to American music. His development had proceeded with a steadiness and an inevitability which foretold fascinating new developments that were never to be realized, although they were already apparent in many of his later piano works. Whatever the eventual judgment on *Treemonisha* (its premiere is projected for early 1972), Joplin's fame is secure in ragtime pieces that are without peer. H. Wiley Hitchcock has described them as "elegant, varied, often subtle, and as sharply incised as a cameo . . . lovely and powerful, infectious and moving."[20]

If the author of this introduction may be allowed the closing privilege of lapsing into the first person singular: may I repeat myself? From one point of view, an all-but-forgotten black-American genius is being honored. From a broader point of view, a country once honored by his life and music is being honored again.

20 *Stereo Review* (April 1971) 84.

Hillforge Farm
July 27 1971

Alternate Covers

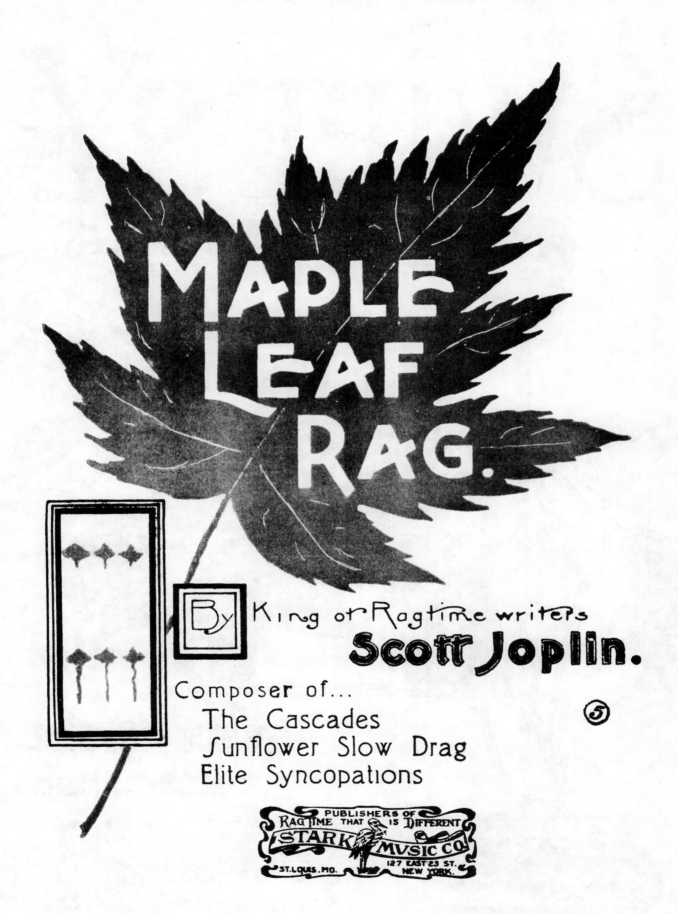

SWIPESY.
CAKE WALK.

BY
SCOTT JOPLIN
AND
ARTHUR MARSHALL.

PUBLISHERS OF
RAGTIME THAT IS DIFFERENT
STARK MUSIC CO.
ST LOUIS MO   127 EAST 23 ST.
NEW YORK

5

Peacherine Rag

BY THE KING OF RAGTIME WRITERS

Scott Joplin

COMPOSER OF

MAPLE LEAF RAG   SWIPSEY CAKE WALK

SUNFLOWER SLOW DRAG   AUGUSTAN CLUB WALTZES

Published By

JOHN STARK & SON

ST. LOUIS, MO.

THE CASCADES

Respectfully Dedicated to
KIMBALL and DONOLLY,
BANJOISTS.

A RAG

THE MASTER PIECE OF *Scott Joplin.*

PUBLISHED BY
JOHN STARK & SON.
ST. LOUIS. MO

Original Works

Dedicated to M. K. & T. Ry.

GREAT CRUSH COLLISION MARCH

By

Scott Joplin.

Author of
"Harmony Club" Waltz. "Combination" March.

Price 40 cents

Published by John R. Fuller

Agent Rob't Smith
Temple, Tex.

Copyright 1896 by John R. Fuller

THE CRUSH COLLISION MARCH.

SCOTT JOPLIN.

Author of "Combintion March"
"Harmony "Club Waltz" &c.

Introd.

PIANO.

Tempo di Marcia.

4.

6

Collision March . 4 .

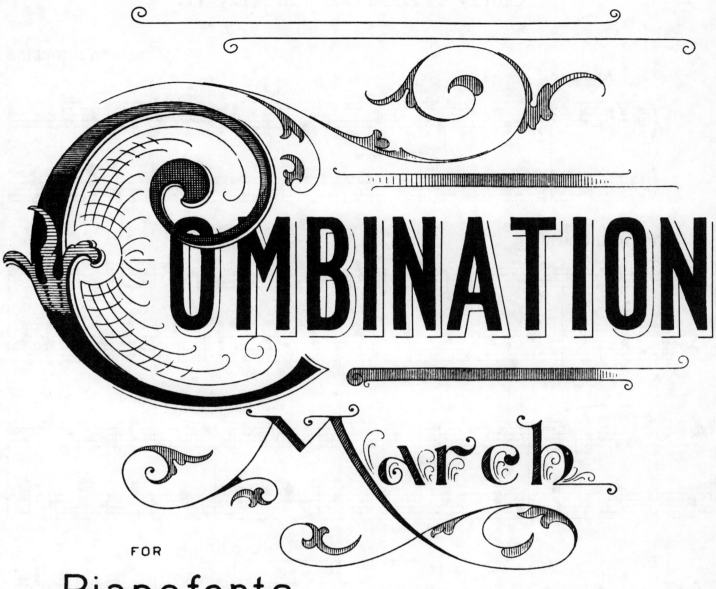

COMBINATION March

FOR

Pianoforte,

by

Scott Joplin,

AUTHOR OF THE CELEBRATED
"HARMONY CLUB WALTZ."

PRICE 40 CENTS.

PUBLISHED BY ROBT. SMITH, TEMPLE, TEX.

LONDON: CHAS. SHEARD & CO.

COMBINATION MARCH.

By SCOTT JOPLIN.

Combination March. 3

Combination March. 3

HARMONY CLUB

COPYRIGHT FOR All Countries.

WALTZ

BY

SCOTT JOPLIN.

Price 40 cents.

PUBLISHED BY ROBT SMITH, TEMPLE, TEX
LONDON, ENG., CHAS. SHEARD & Co.

HARMONY CLUB WALTZ.

INTRO.

By SCOTT JOPLIN.

Andante

WALTZ.

Harmony Club Waltz. 4

16

Harmony Club Waltz. 4

Harmony Club Waltz.4

ORIGINAL RAGS.

Picked by
SCOTT JOPLIN.

Arranged by
CHAS. N. DANIELS.

Copyright 1899 by Carl Hoffman.

Original Rags. 4

Original Rags. 4

MAPLE LEAF RAG.

BY SCOTT JOPLIN.

Tempo di marcia.

TRIO.

PEACHERINE RAG

BY
THE KING OF RAGTIME WRITERS
SCOTT JOPLIN

Composer of
Swipesy Cake Walk
Maple Leaf Rag
Sunflower Slow Drag
Augustan Club Waltzes.

PUBLISHED BY
JOHN STARK & SON
ST. LOUIS, U.S.A.

PEACHERINE RAG.

by **SCOTT JOPLIN**.

Not too fast.

4 — 4

Peacherine Rag.

32

Peacherine Rag.

4—4

Peacherine Rag.

AUGUSTAN CLUB WALTZ.

BY

SCOTT JOPLIN.

Composer of

" Maple Leaf Rag "
" Swipesy Cake Walk "
" Sunflower Slow Drag "

Published by

JOHN STARK & SON

St. Louis, Mo.

THE AUGUSTAN CLUB.

WALTZES.

Composed by
SCOTT JOPLIN.

INTRODUCTION.
Moderato.

36

38

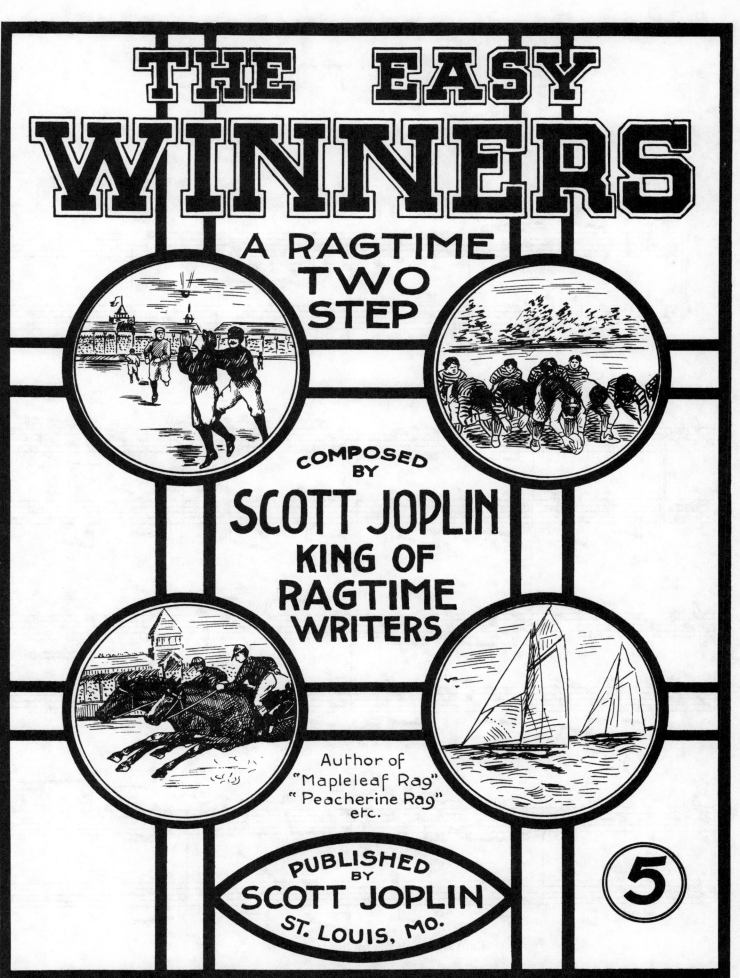

THE EASY WINNERS

A RAGTIME TWO STEP

COMPOSED BY

SCOTT JOPLIN

KING OF RAGTIME WRITERS

Author of
"Mapleleaf Rag"
"Peacherine Rag"
etc.

PUBLISHED BY
SCOTT JOPLIN
ST. LOUIS, MO.

5

"THE EASY WINNERS"

A RAG TIME TWO STEP.

By SCOTT JOPLIN.

Introduction.
Not fast.

Winners. 4.

44

Winners.

Winners. 4.

"CLEOPHA."

MARCH AND TWO-STEP.

SCOTT JOPLIN.

51

The "Conductor." 4.

A BREEZE FROM ALABAMA

A RAGTIME TWO STEP
BY
SCOTT JOPLIN
50¢

DEDECATED TO
P. G. LOWERY
WORLD'S CHALLENGING COLORED
CORNETIST AND BAND MASTER

John Stark & Son
SHEET MUSIC PUBLISHERS
ST. LOUIS

COMPOSER OF
MAPLE LEAF RAG
SUNFLOWER SLOW DRAG
PEACHERINE RAG
SWIPSEY CAKE WALK
THE ENTERTAINER
THE RAG TIME DANCE
AUGUSTAN CLUB WALTZ

A BREEZE FROM ALABAMA.

MARCH AND TWO-STEP.

SCOTT JOPLIN.

Not fast.

A Breeze from Alabama.

A Breeze from Alabama.

A Breeze from Alabama.

ELITE SYNCOPATIONS.

Not fast.

By SCOTT JOPLIN.

62

Dedicated to James Brown and his Mandolin Club.

THE ENTERTAINER.

A RAG TIME TWO STEP.

INTRO:
Not fast.

BY SCOTT JOPLIN.

10 — 4

Copyright 1902 by John Stark & Son.

Repeat 8va.

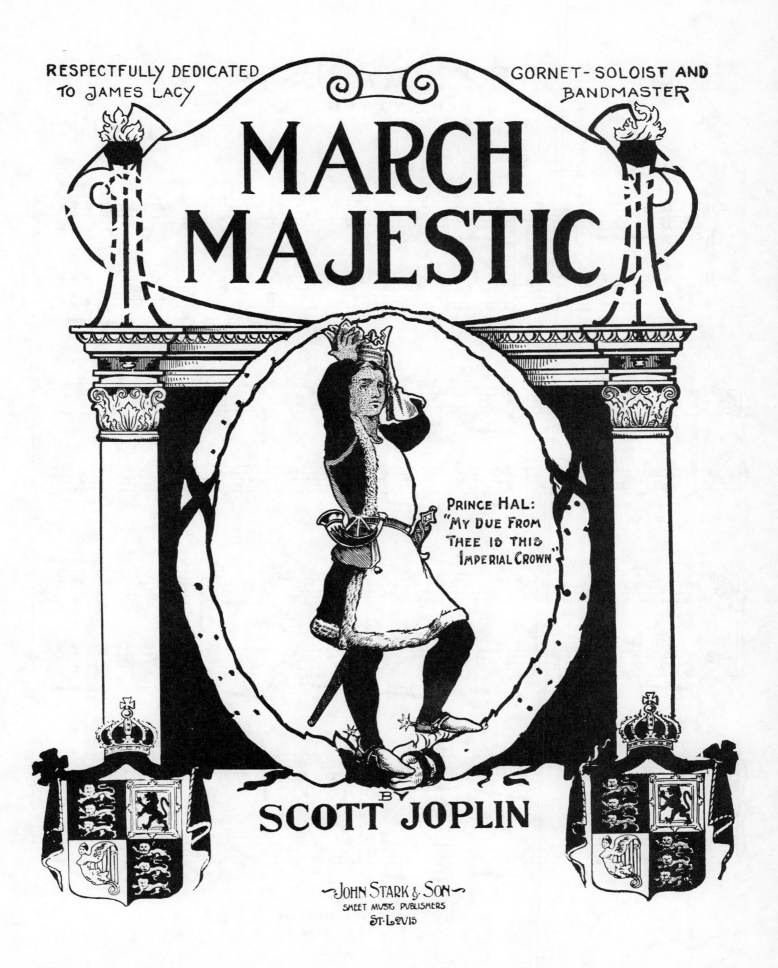

MARCH MAJESTIC.
MARCH AND TWO-STEP.

By SCOTT JOPLIN.

Tempo di marcia.

35 — 4

35 — 4

The Strenuous Life.

A RAGTIME TWO STEP

BY

SCOTT JOPLIN

John Stark & Son
SHEET MUSIC PUBLISHERS
St. Louis

5

THE STRENUOUS LIFE,

A RAGTIME TWO STEP.

BY SCOTT JOPLIN.

Not fast.

5—4

Copyright *1902* by John Stark & Son.

S.L. 4. 5—4

Respectfully Dedicated to the
"PAWNEE CLUB"
ST LOUIS, MO.

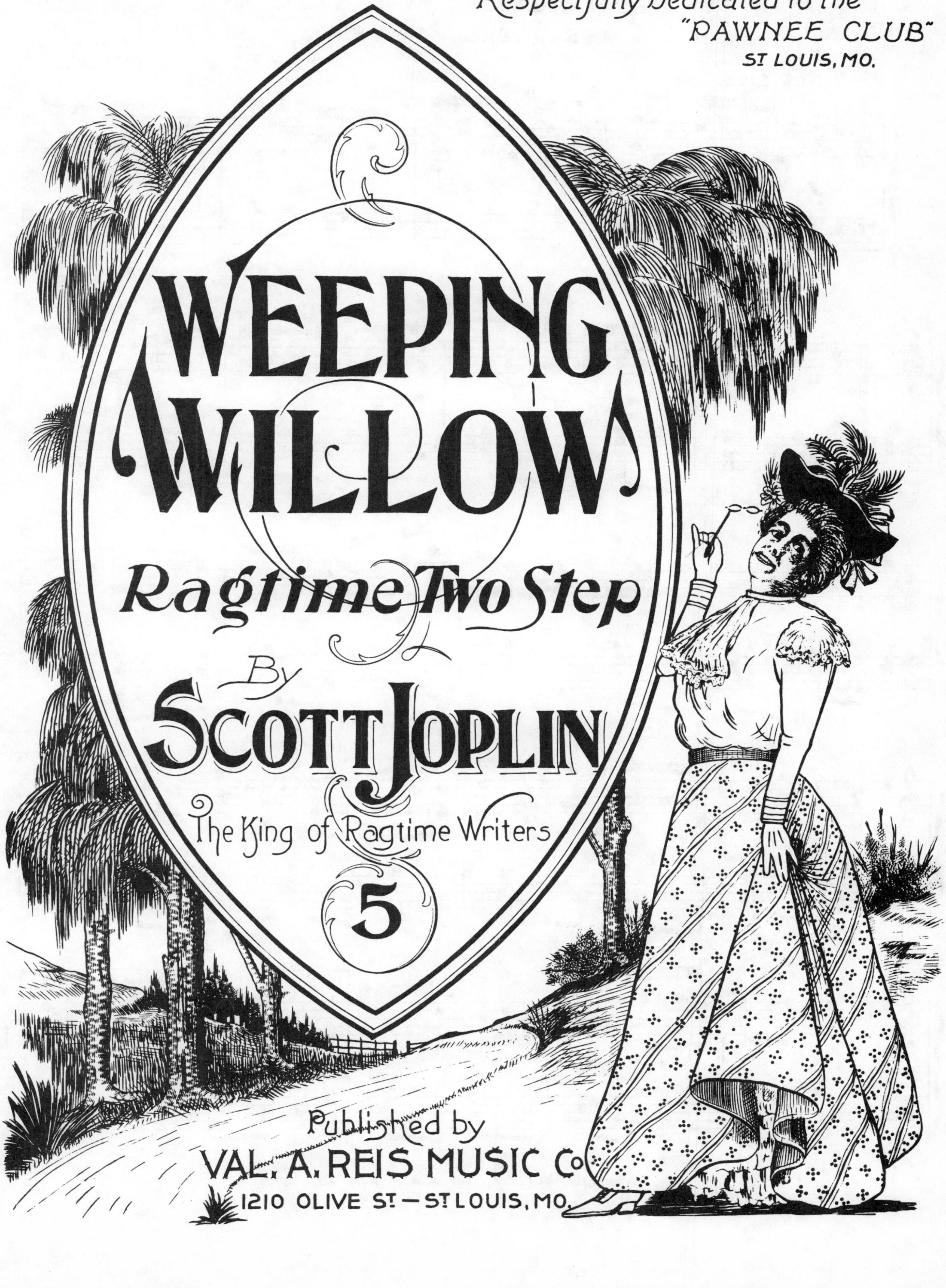

WEEPING WILLOW.

A Rag Time Two Step.

SCOTT JOPLIN.

Not fast.

Palm Leaf Rag

A SLOW DRAG.

By

SCOTT JOPLIN.

The king of ragtime writers
Composer of
~ MAPLE LEAF RAG ~

LONDON, ENG.
CHAS SHEARD
& CO.

VICTOR
KREMER CO.
PUBLISHERS
CHICAGO, NEW YORK

TORONTO, CAN
WHALEY ROYCE
& CO

PALM LEAF RAG

SCOTT JOPLIN
Composer of "Maple Leaf Rag"

Play a little slow

Palm Leaf Rag 3

Palm Leaf Rag 3

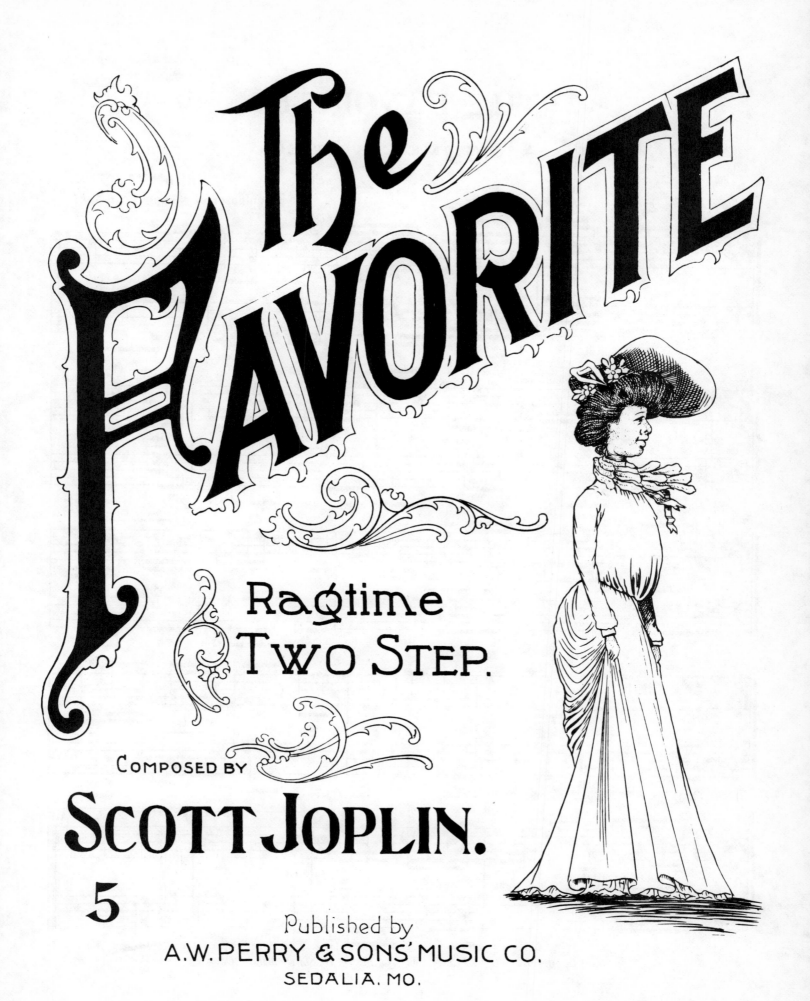

The Favorite

Ragtime Two Step.

Composed by

Scott Joplin.

5

Published by
A.W. Perry & Sons' Music Co.
Sedalia, Mo.

"THE FAVORITE".

A RAGTIME TWO-STEP.

By SCOTT JOPLIN.
Composer of "Maple Leaf Rag".

"The Favorite". 3

Ped.

"The Favorite".4

Dedicated to Minnie L. Montgomery

THE SYCAMORE

A CONCERT RAG

by

SCOTT JOPLIN

Composer of the famous

MAPLE LEAF RAG

5

Published for
BAND.
ORCHESTRA.
MANDOLIN.
GUITAR. ETC.

WILL ROSSITER.
PUBLISHER
New York · Chicago.

Copyright MCMIV by WILL ROSSITER

"THE SYCAMORE."

A CONCERT RAG.

By Scott Joplin.
Composer of "Maple Leaf Rag", etc.

"The Sycamore." 3.

100

"The Sycamore." 3.

THE CASCADES.

A RAG.

Tempo di Marcia.

SCOTT JOPLIN.
Composer of "Maple Leaf Rag."

The Chrysanthemum

AN AFRO-INTERMEZZO

By Scott Joplin.

PUBLISHED BY JOHN STARK & SON. St. Louis Mo.

5

THE CHRYSANTHEMUM.

An Afro-American Intermezzo.

By SCOTT JOPLIN.
Composer of "Maple Leaf Rag."

Slow March Tempo.

9—4

Chrysanthemum. 4. 9—4

110

Chrysanthemum. 4. 9—4

RESPECTFULLY DEDICATED TO MR & MRS. DAN E. DAVENPORT OF ST. LOUIS MO.

BETHENA
A CONCERT WALTZ

BY

SCOTT JOPLIN

COMPOSER OF MAPLE LEAF RAG, CASCADES ETC.

⑤

T. Bahnsen Piano Manufacturing Company

FACTORY & SALESROOMS 1522 OLIVE ST.

"BETHENA"

A CONCERT WALTZ.

By SCOTT JOPLIN.
Composer of "Maple Leaf Rag"

Bethena. 6.

116

Cantabile.

Bethena 6

Cantabile.

Bethena. 6.

Bethena. 6.

Bethena. 6.

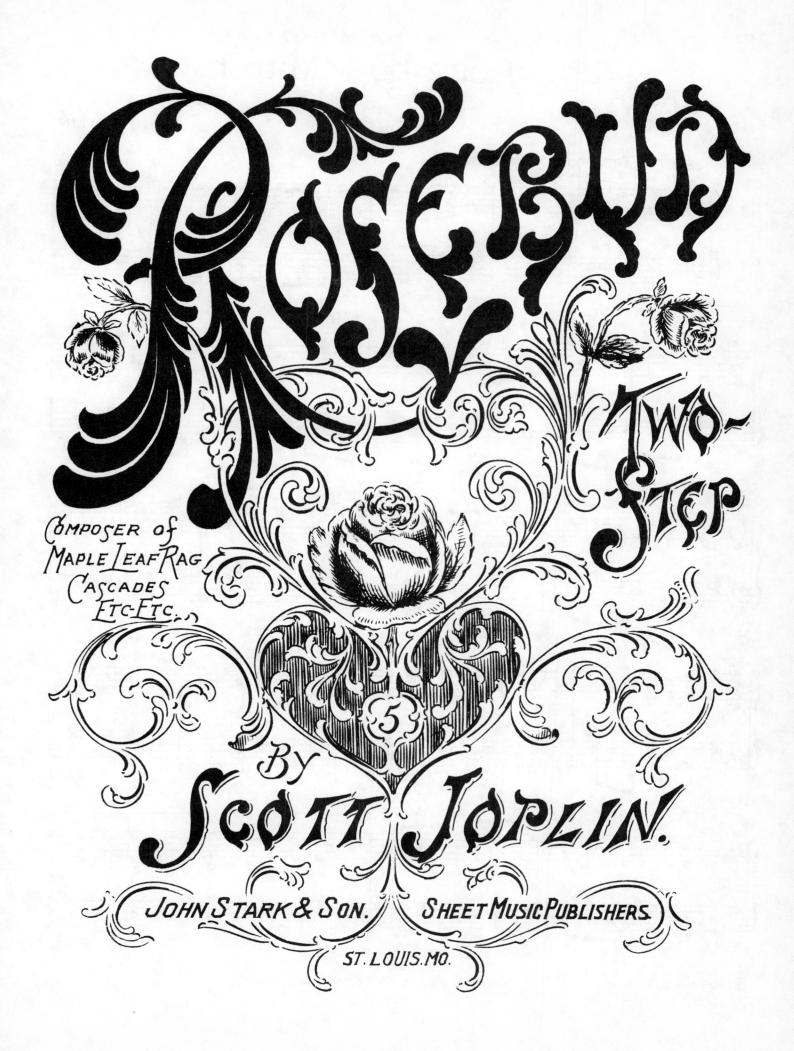

Respectfully dedicated to my friend Tom Turpin.

The Rose-bud March.

SCOTT JOPLIN.

Tempo di Marcia.

88—3
Copyright 1905 by John Stark & Son.

The Rose-bud M. 3

88—3

The Rose-bud M. 3

88-3

Fine.

Respectfully dedicated to Miss Minnie Wade.

LEOLA.
Two-Step.

SCOTT JOPLIN.
Composer of
"Maple Leaf Rag"
"Binks' Waltz" Etc.

Notice! Don't play this piece fast. It is never right to play "rag-time" fast. Author

Slow march tempo.

Leola. 4

Binks' Waltz

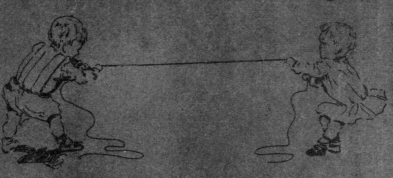

BY

SCOTT JOPLIN

COMPOSER OF
MAPLE LEAF RAG & BETHENA

BAHNSEN MUSIC CO.
1522 OLIVE ST.
ST. LOUIS.

Binks' Waltz.

SCOTT JOPLIN.
"Maple Leaf Rag"
Composer of "Cascades" Etc.

33

Binks'Waltz-6

134

Binks' Waltz.-6

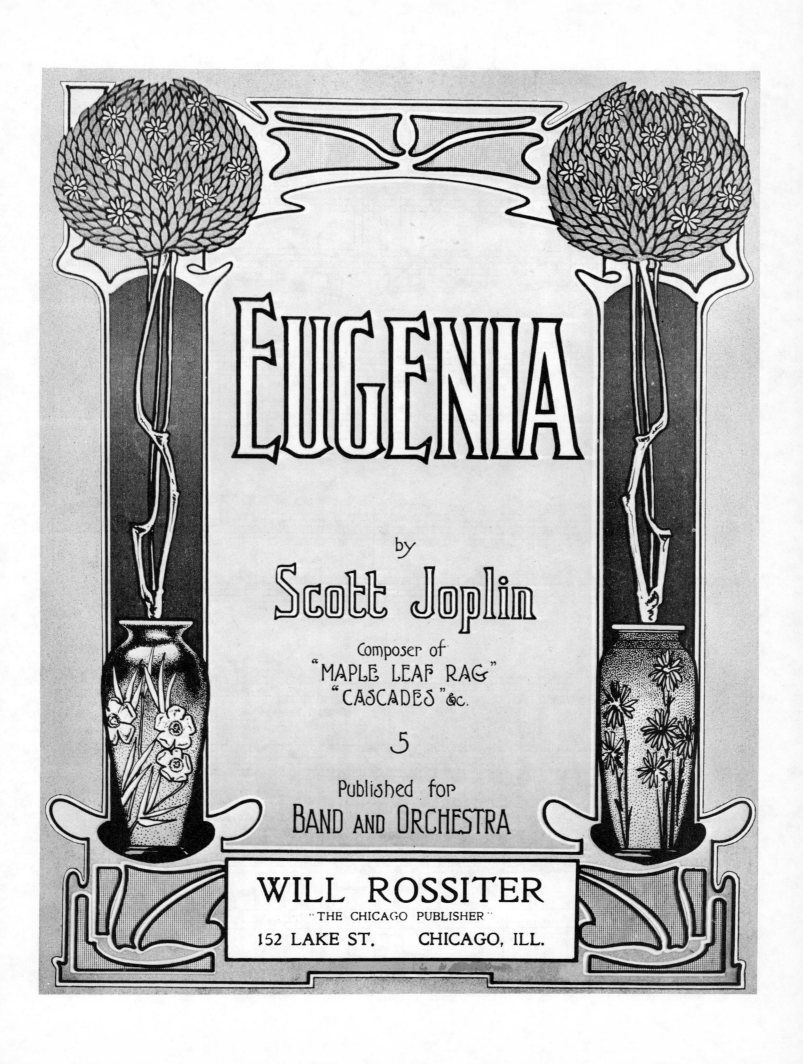

EUGENIA.

Notice.! Dont play this piece fast,
It is never right to play "Ragtime" fast.
Author.

By SCOTT JOPLIN.
Composer of ("Maple Leaf Rag"
("Cascades" etc.

Slow March Tempo ♩ = 72

Eugenia - 4

142

ANTOINETTE

MARCH AND TWO-STEP

COMPOSER OF
MAPLE LEAF RAG
CASCADES
CHRYSANTHEMUM
ETC ETC

By

5

Scott Joplin

PUBLISHERS OF
RAGTIME THAT IS DIFFERENT
STARK MUSIC CO.
ST. LOUIS, MO.   127 EAST 23 ST.
NEW YORK

Respectfully dedicated to Marie Antoinette Williams.

Antoinette.

March and Two-Step.

SCOTT JOPLIN
Composer of "Maple Leaf Rag" etc.

Tempo di Marcia

Copyright, 1906, by Stark Music Printing & Pub. Co.

TRIO.

Rag-Time Dance
A Stop-Time Two Step

By SCOTT JOPLIN

36—4

Copyright MCMVI by John Stark and Son

Ragtime Dance 36-4

154

NOTICE: To get the desired effect of "Stop Time," the pianist will please <u>Stamp</u> the heel of one foot heavily upon the floor at the word "Stamp." Do not raise the toe from the floor while stamping.

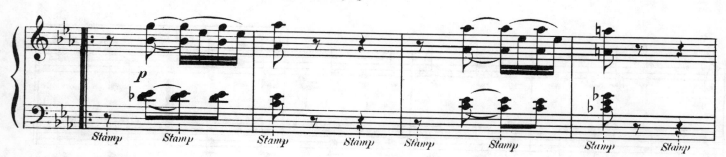

Ragtime Dance 36 — 4

Ragtime Dance 36-4

HOUNSLOW N.Y.

Gladiolus Rag.

Note: Do not play this piece fast
It is never right to play "Ragtime" fast.
Composer.

By SCOTT JOPLIN
Composer of "Maple Leaf Rag"

Slow march tempo.

Piano.

Respectfully dedicated to Miss Mildred Ponder.

THE NONPAREIL.

A Rag & Two Step.

NOTICE: Do not play this piece fast.
It is never right to play "Ragtime" fast.
Author.

SCOTT JOPLIN.
Composer of "Maple Leaf Rag," etc.

Slow march tempo.

45—4

Copyright MCMVII by Stark Music Printing and Publishing Co.

The Nonpareil.- 4

45—4

"SUGAR CANE"
A Ragtime Two Step

NOTE – Do not play this piece fast. It is never right to play Ragtime fast. Composer.

By SCOTT JOPLIN
Composer of "Maple Leaf Rag"

Sugar Cane

Sugar Cane

Sugar Cane

Fine.

PINE APPLE RAG

BY— THE KING OF RAG TIME WRITERS.

SCOTT JOPLIN.

5 Composer of "MAPLE LEAF RAG". "SUGAR CANE RAG". Etc. Etc.

SEMINARY MUSIC Co.
112 WEST 38th ST.
NEW YORK.

Respectfully dedicated to the Five Musical Spillers.

"Pine Apple Rag"

NOTE: Do not play this piece fast.
Composer.

By SCOTT JOPLIN
Composer of "Maple Leaf Rag," and "Sugar Cane Rag."

Pine Apple Rag 4

Pine Apple Rag 4

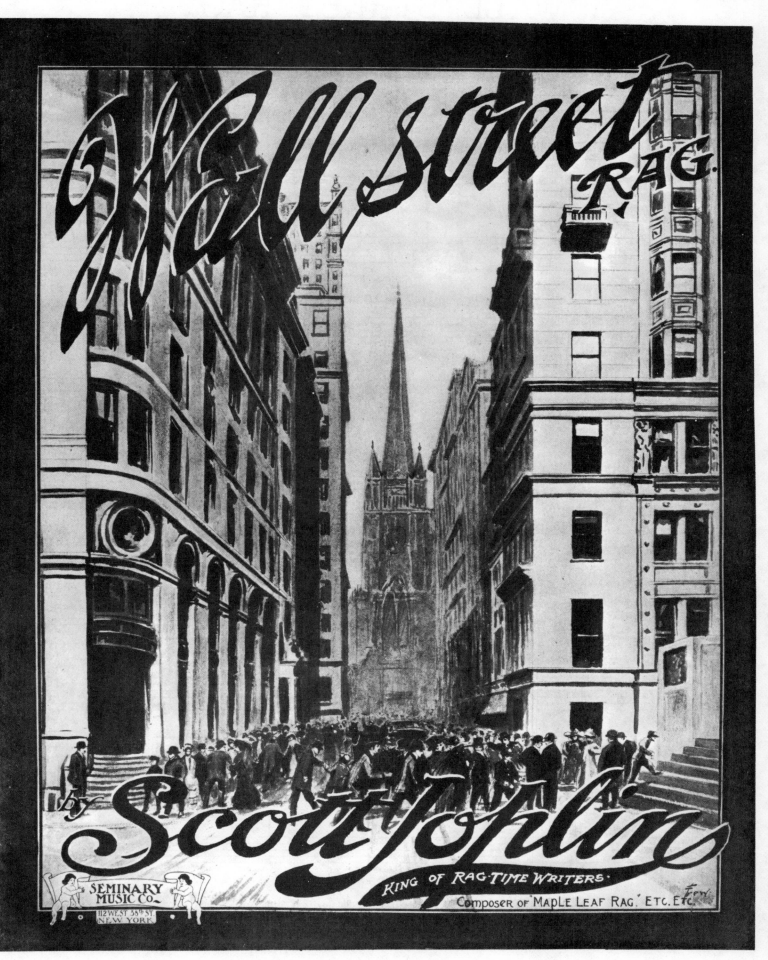

182

WALL STREET "RAG"

NOTE: Do not play this piece fast.
It is never right to play Ragtime fast.
Composer.

By SCOTT JOPLIN
Composer of "Maple Leaf Rag," "Sugar Cane Rag"
and "Pineapple Rag."

Very Slow March Time

PIANO.

Panic in Wall Street, Brokers feeling melancholy.

Good times coming.

Good times have come.

Wall Street Rag

Listening to the strains of genuine negro

ragtime, brokers forget their cares.

Fine.

Wall Street Rag

SOLACE

A MEXICAN SERENADE,

by

SCOTT JOPLIN

SEMINARY MUSIC CO.
112 WEST 38TH ST.
NEW YORK.

"SOLACE"
A Mexican Serenade.

By SCOTT JOPLIN
Composer of "Maple Leaf Rag"

Solace

Solace

Solace

"PLEASANT MOMENTS"

Ragtime Waltz

By SCOTT JOPLIN
Composer of "Maple Leaf Rag"

Pleasant Moment. 4

194

Pleasant Moments. 4

COUNTRY CLUB
RAG TIME TWO-STEP
By The King of Rag Time Writers
SCOTT JOPLIN
COMPOSER OF
MAPLE LEAF RAG.
SUGAR CANE RAG.
PINE APPLE RAG ETC.
SEMINARY MUSIC Co.
112 WEST 38th ST.
NEW YORK.

COUNTRY CLUB.

Ragtime Two Step

NOTE: Do not play this piece fast.
It is never right to play Ragtime fast.
Composer.

By SCOTT JOPLIN.
Composer of "Maple Leaf Rag," "Sugar Cane Rag"
and "Pineapple Rag."

Slow March Time.

PIANO.

Our latest Seminary Illustrated Thematic Catalogue to be had at any first-
class Music Store, or will be mailed free upon receipt of a Postal Card.
Seminary Music Co. 112 W. 38th St. N.Y.

Country Club 4

200

Country Club 4

EUPHONIC SOUNDS
A SYNCOPATED NOVELTY

SCOTT JOPLIN

BY
SCOTT JOPLIN
KING OF RAGTIME WRITERS
COMPOSER OF
MAPLE LEAF RAG, PINEAPPLE RAG, SUGAR CANE RAG,
COUNTRY CLUB RAG, ETC

SEMINARY
MUSIC CO
112 WEST 38th ST.
NEW YORK.

Euphonic Sounds.

A SYNCOPATED TWO STEP.

NOTE. Do not play this piece fast.
It is never right to play Ragtime fast.
Composer.

By SCOTT JOPLIN,
Composer of "Maple Leaf Rag," "Sugar Cane Rag,"
"Wall Street Rag" and "Pineapple Rag," etc.

Slow March time

Piano.

206

Fine.

SOMETHING NEW !!!

"CUPID'S KISS" WALTZ,

By the Composer of "Kiss Of Spring" Waltz.

RESPECTFULLY DEDICATED TO THE C.V.B.A.

PARAGON
RAG

BY THE KING OF RAG TIME WRITERS
SCOTT JOPLIN
COMPOSER OF

MAPLE LEAF RAG
PINE APPLE RAG
SUGAR CANE RAG
COUNTRY CLUB RAG
WALL STREET RAG ETC

SEMINARY
MUSIC CO.
112 WEST 38TH ST
NEW YORK

5

Respectfully Dedicated to the C.V.B.A.

PARAGON RAG

By SCOTT JOPLIN,
Composer of "Maple Leaf Rag," "Sugar Cane Rag,"
"Wall Street Rag" and "Pineapple Rag."

Slow March Time

Copyright 1909 by Seminary Music Co. 112 W. 38th St. N.Y.

Paragon Rag 5

Trio.

Paragon Rag 5

STOPTIME RAG

BY
SCOTT·JOPLIN
COMPOSER OF
"GLADIOLUS·RAG"
"SEARCHLIGHT·RAG"

Published by JOS. W. STERN & CO

"Stoptime"
Rag.

To get the desired effect of "Stoptime" the pianist should stamp the heel
of one foot heavily upon the floor, wherever the word "Stamp" appears in the music.

by SCOTT JOPLIN.

Composer of { Gladionlus Rag.
{ Searchlight Rag.

Fast or slow.

218

219

6490-4

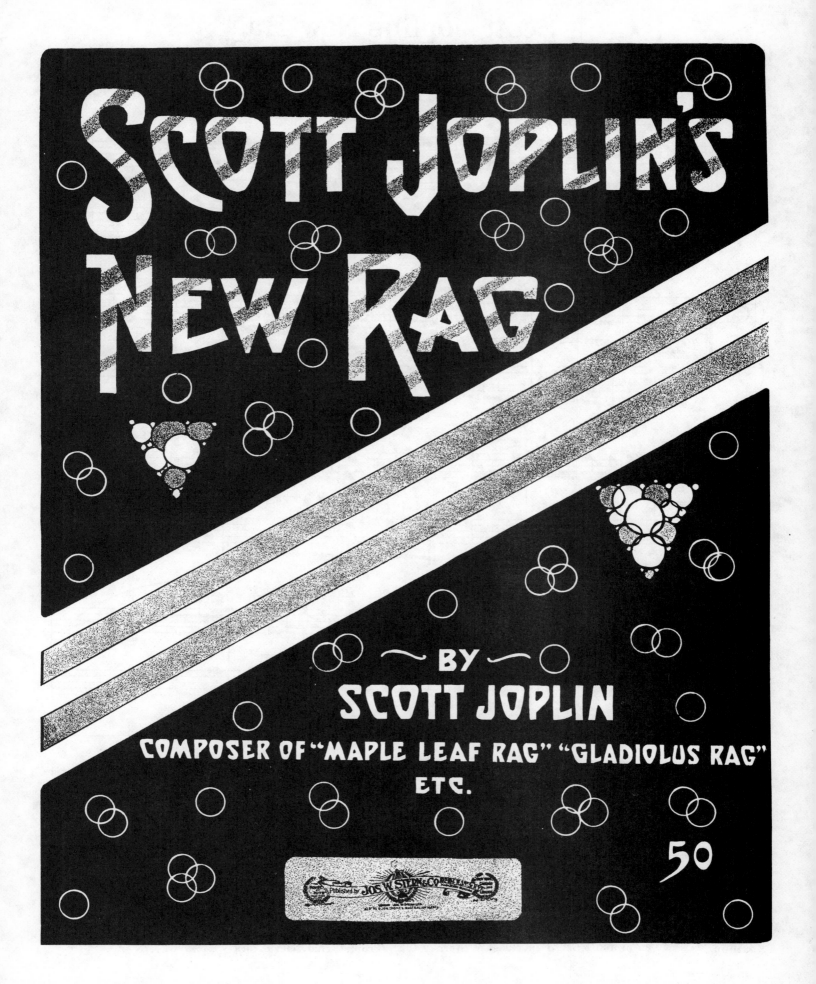

Scott Joplin's New Rag

By SCOTT JOPLIN

Allegro moderato.

Magnetic Rag

BY

Scott Joplin

Composer of
MAPLE LEAF RAG
EUPHONIC SOUNDS
Etc.

— ❦ 5 ❦ —

Scott Joplin Music Publishing Co.
NEW YORK, N.Y.

MAGNETIC RAG

by SCOTT JOPLIN
Composer of "Maple Leaf Rag"

Allegretto ma non troppo

Magnetic Rag. 5

230

Tempo l'istesso

Magnetic Rag. 3

Magnetic Rag. 3

Reflection Rag
(SYNCOPATED MUSINGS)

SCOTT JOPLIN

Slow March Tempo.

Reflection Rag, 2.

Collaborative Works

SWIPESY.

CAKE   WALK.

BY SCOTT JOPLIN
AND
ARTHUR MARSHALL.

Scott Joplin   Arthur Marshall

Published by

5

John Stark & Son.

ST. LOUIS

"SWIPESY"

CAKE WALK.

By SCOTT JOPLIN
and
ARTHUR MARSHALL.

Swipsey. 4.

Swipesy. 4.

Swipesy. 4.

A RAG TIME TWO-STEP.

SUNFLOWER SLOW DRAG.

BY

SCOTT JOPLIN & SCOTT HAYDEN

Scott Joplin. Composer of
"Maple Leaf Rag."
"Swipesy Cake Walk."
"Aqustain Club Waltz."

Published by

JOHN STARK & SON
ST. LOUIS

SUN FLOWER SLOW DRAG.

RAG TIME TWO STEP.

By SCOTT JOPLIN
and
SCOTT HAYDEN.

INTRO.
Not fast.

2 – 4

Sun flower. 4.

2—4

248

Sunflower. 4.   2—1

2—4

SOMETHING

DOING

Cake Walk MARCH

BY *Scott Joplin* AND *Scott Hayden*

PUBLISHED BY

VAL A. REIS MUSIC CO.

1210 OLIVE ST.   ST. LOUIS MO.

"Something Doing."

A RAGTIME TWO STEP.

SCOTT JOPLIN
SCOTT HAYDEN.

Intro.
Not fast.

Copyright, MCMIII, by Val. A. Reis Music Co.
St. Louis, Mo.

S. D. 4

Lily Queen
a Ragtime Two-Step
By
ARTHUR MARSHALL
COMPOSER OF "SWIPSEY CAKEWALK"
AND "KINKLETS
AND
SCOTT JOPLIN
COMPOSER OF "MAPLE LEAF"
AND "WEEPING WILLOW"
PUBLISHED BY
W. W. STUART, 48 W. 28TH ST. NEW YORK
5

"LILY QUEEN."
A Ragtime Two-Step.

By SCOTT JOPLIN
and ARTHUR MARSHALL.

NOTE: Do not play this piece fast.
It is never right to play "Ragtime" fast. Composers.

Moderato.

1 = 4

"Lily Queen". 1 = 4

260

"Lily Queen." **1** = **4**

"Lily Queen." 1 = 4

BY
SCOTT JOPLIN,
&
LOUIS CHAUVIN,

Heliotrope Bouquet.

A SLOW DRAG TWO-STEP

5

PUBLISHERS OF
RAG TIME THAT IS DIFFERENT
STARK MVSIC CO.
ST. LOUIS. MO.   127 EAST 23 ST.
NEW YORK.

HELIOTROPE BOUQUET
A Slow Drag Two Step.

*N.B. Do not play this piece
fast. It is never right to
play "Ragtime" fast. Composers.*

By SCOTT JOPLIN
and LOUIS CHAUVIN.

Heliotrope Bouquet. 4

266

Heliotrope Bouquet. 4

Heliotrope Bouquet. 4

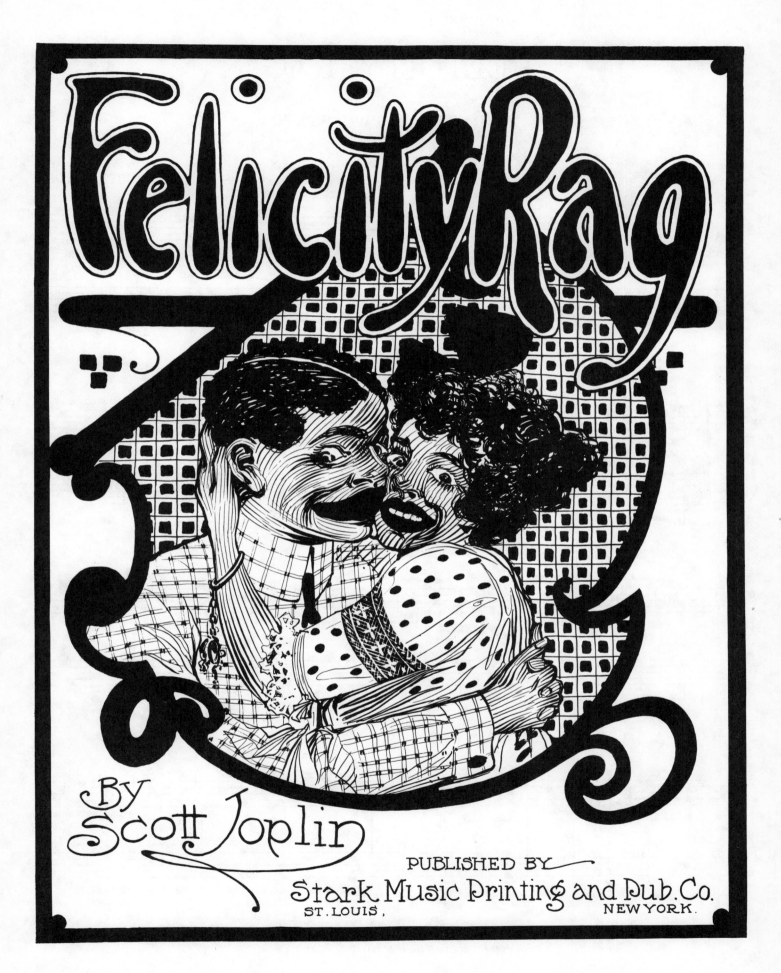

FELICITY RAG.

A RAGTIME TWO STEP.

SCOTT JOPLIN
and
SCOTT HAYDEN.

Tempo di Marcia.

Copyright 1911 by Stark Music Ptg. & Pub. Co.

Kismet Rag.

By SCOTT JOPLIN
and SCOTT HAYDEN.

INTRO.

Not fast.

Kismet Rag, 4.

Kismet Rag, 4.

Kismet Rag, 4.

Miscellaneous Works

School of Ragtime

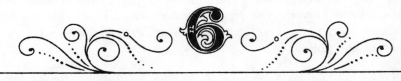

6

EXERCISES

FOR

PIANO

BY

SCOTT JOPLIN.

Composer of "MAPLE LEAF RAG" *etc.*

Price 50 cents.

NEW YORK
Published by **SCOTT JOPLIN.**

SCHOOL OF RAGTIME

BY

SCOTT JOPLIN

Composer of "Maple Leaf Rag."

REMARKS— What is scurrilously called ragtime is an invention that is here to stay. That is now conceded by all classes of musicians. That all publications masquerading under the name of ragtime are not the genuine article will be better known when these exercises are studied. That real ragtime of the higher class is rather difficult to play is a painful truth which most pianists have discovered. Syncopations are no indication of light or trashy music, and to shy bricks at "hateful ragtime" no longer passes for musical culture. To assist amateur players in giving the "Joplin Rags" that weird and intoxicating effect intended by the composer is the object of this work.

Exercise No. 1.

It is evident that, by giving each note its proper time and by scrupulously observing the ties, you will get the effect. So many are careless in these respects that we will specify each feature. In this number, strike the first note and hold it through the time belonging to the second note. The upper staff is not syncopated, and is not to be played. The perpendicular dotted lines running from the syncopated note below to the two notes above will show exactly its duration. Play slowly until you catch the swing, and never play ragtime fast at any time.

Slow march tempo (*Count Two*)

Exercise No. 2.

This style is rather more difficult, especially for those who are careless with the left hand, and are prone to vamp. The first note should be given the full length of three sixteenths, and no more. The second note is struck in its proper place and the third note is not struck but is joined with the second as though they were one note. This treatment is continued to the end of the exercise.

Slow march tempo (*Count Two*)

English Copyright Secured.　　　　Copyright MCMVIII by Scott Joplin.

Exercise No. 3.

This style is very effective when neatly played. If you have observed the object of the dotted lines they will lead you to a proper rendering of this number and you will find it interesting.

Exercise No. 4.

The fourth and fifth notes here form one tone, and also in the middle of the second measure and so to the end. You will observe that it is a syncopation only when the tied notes are on the same degree of the staff. Slurs indicate a legato movement.

Exercise No. 5.

The first ragtime effect here is the second note, right hand, but, instead of a tie, it is an eighth note: rather than two sixteenths with tie. In the last part of this measure, the tie is used because the tone is carried across the bar. This is a pretty style and not as difficult as it seems on first trial.

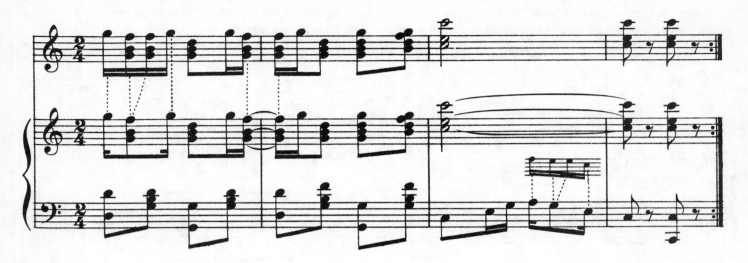

Exercise No.6.

The instructions given, together with the dotted lines, will enable you to interpret this variety which has very pleasing effects. We wish to say here, that the "Joplin ragtime" is destroyed by careless or imperfect rendering, and very often good players lose the effect entirely, by playing too fast. They are harmonized with the supposition that each note will be played as it is written, as it takes this and also the proper time divisions to complete the sense intended.

Slow march tempo (*Count Two*)

Respectfully inscribed to Miss Nellie M. Buttler.

SENSATION.
A Rag.

JOSEPH F. LAMB.
Arr by Scott Joplin

Tempo di marcia.

Trio.

SILVER SWAN RAG

Attributed to

SCOTT JOPLIN.

SILVER SWAN RAG

Slow March Tempo

Attributed to SCOTT JOPLIN

292

Fine.

Appendixes

ROLLOGRAPHY OF JOPLIN WORKS

The following list was mainly derived from the Joplin rollography compiled by Michael Montgomery, published in Record Research *(Apr-May 1959), and from the list of player piano rolls in the Blesh/Janis book* They All Played Ragtime *(third edition, 1966). Information about* Silver Swan Rag *was supplied by QRS Music Rolls, Inc. Unless otherwise indicated, all piano rolls were mechanically cut. Asterisks denote rolls played by Joplin. Ole Miss Rag by W. C. Handy is appended to the list for its interest as the only known recording by Joplin of music by another composer.*

THE CASCADES
Connorized 430
—854 (in medley)
—4172
—6047
QRS 30088

THE CHRYSANTHEMUM
Connorized 6076

THE ENTERTAINER
Cecilian 6046
Connorized 6046
QRS x3087
—30358

EUPHONIC SOUNDS (in medleys)
Angelus 90193
Metrostyle 102302
Universal 77987
—92715

THE FAVORITE
Connorized 4173
QRS x3345

FELICITY RAG [with Scott Hayden]
Kimball B6781
U. S. Music 65050B

FIG LEAF RAG
QRS 03073
—30141

GLADIOLUS RAG
American Piano Co 12623
Angelus 90002
Electra 76896
Kimball c6529
Metro Style Themodist 79513
—92261
QRS 30162
Standard 76836
Universal 92265
—77769D

KISMET RAG [with Scott Hayden]
Kimball B6793
U. S. Music 5819

MAGNETIC RAG
*Connorized 10266

MAPLE LEAF RAG
Aeolian Grand 8440
American Piano Co 493
—4066 (in medley)
—95101
Angelus 90080
Artempo 9976 (played by
    Steve Williams)
Arto 8440
Capitol 95101
Connorized 148
—2966 (in medley)
—4028
*—10265
Kimball F6154 (in medley)
Melographic 0369
—1731
Mel-O-Dee 89965
*Metro Art 202704
Metro Style Themodist 89961
Perfection 8440
QRS x3817
—7308 (played by J. L. Cook)
—30900
—100419 (played by
    Max Kortlander)
Starr Piano Co 8057
Supertone 10029
*Uni-Record Melody 202705
Universal 8440
—89965
U. S. Music 1368
—61368B
—65399F (in medley)

NONPAREIL (None to Equal)
Connorized 4401

ORIGINAL RAGS
Aeolian Grand 20428
Automusic Perforating Co 4051
Connorized 843

—4051
Melographic 0370
QRS 3268

PALM LEAF RAG
QRS x3034
—30342

PARAGON RAG
U. S. Music 75378 (in medley)

PEACHERINE RAG
Connorized 6047

PINE APPLE RAG (in medleys)
Angelus 90193
Lyon & Healy 6067
Metrostyle 102303
Universal 77987
—92715

PLEASANT MOMENTS
*Connorized (number unknown)

THE RAGTIME DANCE
QRS x3626

ROSE LEAF RAG
Connorized 1336

SCOTT JOPLIN'S NEW RAG
Aeolian Grand (number unknown)
American Piano Co 11263
Angelus 90806
Connorized 2121
Kimball c 6132
Metro Style Themodist 99362
QRS 31282
Starr Piano Co (number unknown)
Universal 79527
—99365

SEARCHLIGHT RAG
QRS x3866
—30595

SILVER SWAN RAG
National (number unknown)
QRS 31533

SOMETHING DOING [with Scott Hayden]
Connorized 4433
*—10278
QRS 30396
Royal 3389
U. S. Music 6055

STOPTIME RAG
QRS 30786

THE STRENUOUS LIFE
Connorized 4090

SUGAR CANE
Connorized 4421

SUNFLOWER SLOW DRAG
[with Scott Hayden]
Aeolian Grand 8479
American Piano Co 1072
Connorized 844
—4082
Universal 8479

SWIPESY—Cake Walk
[with Arthur Marshall]
Connorized 4087
QRS 30328

THE SYCAMORE
Connorized 4320
QRS 30395

WALL STREET RAG
Master Record 653

WEEPING WILLOW
Connorized 400
—4411
*—10277
QRS 30404

OLE MISS RAG [W. C. Handy]
*Connorized 10304

DISCOGRAPHY OF 78 rpm RECORDS OF JOPLIN WORKS

The following list was compiled by David A. Jasen.

THE CASCADES
Wally Rose / Good Time Jazz 27 / June 1950
Ralph Sutton / Down Home 10 / Nov 1949

THE CHRYSANTHEMUM
Mutt Carey's Jazz Band / Century 4008 / Nov 1947

THE EASY WINNERS
Nap Hayes & Matthew Prater / Okeh 45314 / Feb 1928
Wally Rose / Good Time Jazz 28 / June 1950
Roy Sturgis / (E) Melodisc 1028 / June 1951
Lu Watters Yerba Buena Jazz Band / West Coast 113 / Feb 1947

THE ENTERTAINER
Mutt Carey's New Yorkers / Century 4007 / Nov 1947
Player-piano Roll / Jazz Classics 534

EUPHONIC SOUNDS
James P. Johnson / Asch 551 / June 1944
Wally Rose / Good Time Jazz 51 / July 1951

FIG LEAF RAG
Player-piano Roll / Jazz Classics 533

GLADIOLUS RAG
Pathé Dance Orchestra / Pathé 29050
Wally Rose / Good Time Jazz 25 / June 1950
Lee Stafford / Castle 11 / Jan 1950

HELIOTROPE BOUQUET [with Louis Chauvin]
Lee Stafford / Castle 10 / Jan 1950

MAPLE LEAF RAG
Danny Alvin's Kings of Dixieland / Rondo 236 / May 1950
Victor Arden & Phil Ohman / Victor 22608 / Dec 1930
Lil Armstrong / (F) Vogue 5169 / May 1953
Marvin Ash / Capitol 15435 / Dec 1949
Sidney Bechet with Claude Luter's Orchestra / (F) Vogue 5039 / Nov 1949
Graeme Bell / (A) Swaggie 4 / March 1950
Graeme Bell / (A) Parlophone A 7824 / Apr 1953
Bluebird Military Band / Bluebird 3201 / Aug 1938
Sune Borg / (Sweden) Gazell 3001 / Oct 1949
Brun Campbell / West Coast 112 / June 1945
Brun Campbell / Brun 1 / 1952
Frankie Carle & Orchestra / Victor 20-3805
Joe Fingers Carr & Band / Capitol 2665 / Aug 1953
Ken Colyer's Jazzmen / (E) Columbia DB 4783 / Nov 1961
*Eddie Condon Orchestra / Decca 27035 Mar 1950
*Tommy Dorsey Orchestra / Victor 25496 / Oct 1936
*Hank Duncan Trio / Black & White 31 / June 1944
*Willie Eckstein / Okeh 40018 / Nov 1923
Bernard Ette & Jazz Kings / (G) Tri-Ergon 5064 / Oct 1927
*Don Ewell / Jazz Limited 101 / Feb 1949
Vera Guilaroff / Pathé 21178 / July 1926
W. G. Haenschen's Banjo Band / Personal M-61070 / 1910
Halfway House Orchestra / Columbia 476-D / Sept 1925

Maple Leaf Rag, continued

    *Earl Hines Orchestra / Decca 218 / Sept 1934

    Art Hodes & Chicagoans / Blue Note 505 / Mar 1944

    Paul Hoffman / (G) Polydor / Sept 1927

    Stig Holm / (G) Telefunken 15050

    Hotcha-Mundharmonika Trio / (G) Phillips P-17155 / 1953

    Parke Hunter / (E) HMV GC 6368 / Oct 1902

    Scott Joplin (Player-piano Roll) / Circle 5003

    Art Lund / MGM 10713

    Humphrey Lytellton Jazz Band / (E) Parlophone 3346

    Paul Mares & Friars Society Orchestra / Okeh 41575 / Jan 1935

    Fabio Mataloni / (Italy) Parlophone TT 9580 / June 1952

    G. G. McBrayer / Champion 20335 / June 1928

    Clyde McCoy & Orchestra / Decca 681 / July 1935

    Deke Moffitt & his Twenty-niners / King 1340

    Max Morath / Gold Camp 105

    *Jelly Roll Morton / Circle 21-22

    Ozzie Nelson Orchestra / Bluebird 7726 / July 1938

    *New Orleans Feetwarmers / Victor 23360 / Sept 1932

    New Orleans Rhythm Kings / Gennet 5104 / Mar 1923

    Old Time Band / Bluebird 7816

    Kid Ory's Creole Jazz Band / Crescent 8 / Nov 1945

    *Vess L. Ossman / Columbia 3626 / Mar 1907 (reissued as Columbia A 228)

    Vess L. Ossman / Imperial 45600 / May 1907

    Knocky Parker Trio / Texstar 200 / 1949

    Ike Ragon Orchestra / Vocalion 03513 / Mar 1937

    J. Russel Robinson / Eagle 900 / released Sept 1947

    Harry Roy Orchestra / (E) Parlophone F 1133 / Dec 1937

    Harry Roy Orchestra (m) / (E) Parlophone F 1568 / Feb 1939

    Elmer Schoebel's Dixieband / National 9113

    Ethel Smith / Decca 27015 / May 1950

    Harry Snodgrass / Brunswick 3239 / Apr 1926

    Ralph Sutton / (Switzerland) Elite Special 9114 / July 1952

    John Scott Trotter Orchestra / Decca 4217

    U. S. Marine Band / Victor 4911 / Oct 1906

    U. S. Marine Band / Victor 16792 / Feb 1909

    Fred Van Eps with Orchestra / Zonophone 5917 / released June 1912

    Fred Van Eps with Piano / V-1 / Mar 1952

    Lu Watters Yerba Buena Jazz Band / Jazz Man 1 / Dec 1941

    Lu Watters Yerba Buena Jazz Band / West Coast 114 / Feb 1947

    Teddy Weatherford / Swing 315 / June 1937

    Herb Wiedoeft's Cinderella Roof Orchestra / Brunswick 2795 / Sept 1924

    Bill Williams & Dixieland Band / Albert 725-1 / Dec 1949

    The Yorkshire Jazz Band / (E) Esquire 32-105 / July 1956

ORIGINAL RAGS

    Sune Borg / (Sweden) Gazell 3001 / Oct 1949

    Jelly Roll Morton / General 4001 / Dec 1939

    Player-piano Roll / Jazz Classics 534

    Wally Rose & Rhythm / West Coast 112 / Feb 1947

PINE APPLE RAG

    Wally Rose / Good Time Jazz 27 / June 1950

    Lu Watters Yerba Buena Jazz Band / West Coast 110 / June 1946

SCOTT JOPLIN'S NEW RAG
  Player-piano Roll / Jazz Classics 533

SUGAR CANE
  Frank Plada's Serenaders / Gennet 6166 / released Aug 1927

SUNFLOWER SLOW DRAG [with Scott Hayden]
  Tony Parenti's Ragtimers / Circle 1029 / Nov 1947
  Player-piano Roll / Circle 5005

SWIPESY—Cake Walk [with Arthur Marshall]
  Eric Brooks / (E) Poydras 17 / 1950
  The Merseysissippi Jazz Band / (E) Esquire 10-438 / Feb 1955
  Tony Parenti's Ragtimers / Circle 1031 / Nov 1947

WALL STREET RAG
  Zonophone Orchestra / Zonophone 5603 / released Mar 1910

WEEPING WILLOW
  Player-piano Roll / Circle 5005

* Included on 33⅓ rpm record *They All Played the Maple Leaf Rag* / Herwin 401 / 1971,
together with these additional recordings:
  Eubie Blake / Private Recording / 1969
  W. C. Handy & Orchestra (called *Fuzzy Wuzzy Rag*) / Columbia A 2421 / 1917
  James P. Johnson / Folkways FJ 2841 (LP)
  Paul Lingle / Euphonic 1203 (LP)
  Willie the Lion Smith / Grand Award 33-368 (LP)

SELECTIVE DISCOGRAPHY OF 33-1/3 rpm
RECORDS OF JOPLIN WORKS

Although his compositions have often been included on long-playing records comprising selections of various composers, only those records devoted entirely or predominantly to Joplin are listed here.

THE BEST OF SCOTT JOPLIN
  Max Morath / Vanguard VSD-39/40 / 1972

THE COMPLETE PIANO WORKS OF SCOTT JOPLIN†
  Professor John W. (Knocky) Parker / Audiophile AP 71-72

AN EVENING WITH SCOTT JOPLIN
  William Bolcom, Joshua Rifkin, Mary Lou Williams, piano
  Barbara Christopher, Clamma Dale, Michael Gordon, Chorus, John Motley / NYPL-SJ / 1972

FIVE CLASSIC RAGS *(reverse side of Selections from Treemonisha, see below)*
  Ann Charters / Portents 3 / 1965

THE GOLDEN AGE OF RAGTIME
  Player-piano Rolls / Riverside RLP 12-110 / 1956

A JOPLIN BOUQUET
  Ann Charters / Portents 1

PIANO RAGS BY SCOTT JOPLIN
  Joshua Rifkin / Nonesuch H-71248B / 1970

PIANO RAGS BY SCOTT JOPLIN, VOLUME II
  Joshua Rifkin / Nonesuch H-71264 / 1972

SCOTT JOPLIN—1916
  Player-piano Rolls (including six played by Joplin) / Biograph BLP-1006Q / 1971

SCOTT JOPLIN RAGTIME, VOLUME 2
  Player-piano Rolls / Biograph BLP-1008Q / 1971

SCOTT JOPLIN—RAGTIME PIONEER
  Player-piano Rolls (some played by Joplin) / (Holland) Riverside RLP 8815

SELECTIONS FROM *Treemonisha*
  Carolyn Lewis, Utah State University Concert Chorale, Ted Puffer / Portents 3 / 1965

THEY ALL PLAYED THE MAPLE LEAF RAG
  Fifteen previously recorded performances / Herwin 401 / 1971 *(see* second Appendix)

† Comparison between this album and the printed scores shows a divergence in musical content: considerable improvisation has been added and repeats are consistently omitted.

Index

The Index covers all works contained in both volumes. Cover titles and subtitles are listed first in each entry. Differing caption titles and/or subtitles for the same work follow. Where only one title is listed, cover and caption title material agree. Owners of original copyrights (in most cases, the publishers) and full dates of registered copyrights are next given. Where copyrights were registered by others than the publishers, the publishers' names follow, with parentheses. A full list of the original publishers and their locations follows the Index. Names of present copyright holders and the works they control will be found in the sections devoted to permissions on the copyright page of each volume. Asterisks indicate works not included in this edition (see Editor's Note, page xi).

Roman numerals refer to the volume and arabic numerals to the page numbers—for example, I:203 means Volume I, page 203.

All references to II apply to the hardcover edition of The Collected Works of Scott Joplin, Volume II: Works for Voice, published by The New York Public Library.

SOMETHING DOING—Cake Walk March   I:251
   Something Doing—A Ragtime Two Step
   [with Scott Hayden]
   Reis, Feb 24 1903

STOPTIME RAG   I:215
   Stern, Jan 4 1910

THE STRENUOUS LIFE—A Ragtime Two Step   I:77
   Stark, 1902
   (No copyright registration recorded)

SUGAR CANE—A Ragtime Classic Two Step   I:169
   Sugar Cane—A Ragtime Two Step
   Seminary, Apr 21 1908

SUNFLOWER SLOW DRAG—A Rag Time Two-Step   I:245
   Sun Flower Slow Drag—Rag Time Two Step
   [with Scott Hayden]
   Stark, Mar 18 1901

SWIPESY—Cake Walk   I:239
   [with Arthur Marshall]
   Stark, July 21 1900

THE SYCAMORE—A Concert Rag   I:97
   Rossiter, July 18 1904

TREEMONISHA—Opera in Three Acts   II:3
   Joplin, May 19 1911
   Revised excerpts:
   —Frolic of the Bears   II:261
      Joplin, June 22 1915
   —Prelude to Act 3   II:255
      Joplin, Dec 15 1913
   —A Real Slow Drag   II:237
      Joplin, July 15 1913

WALL STREET RAG   I:181
   Seminary, Feb 23 1909

WEEPING WILLOW—Ragtime Two Step   I:83
   Weeping Willow—A Rag Time Two Step
   Reis, June 6 1903

WHEN YOUR HAIR IS LIKE THE SNOW   II:319
   Words by Owen Spendthrift
   Spendthrift, May 18 1907

ORIGINAL PUBLISHERS

American Music Syndicate, St Louis
T. Bahnsen Piano Mfg Co, St Louis
   (also Bahnsen Music Co, St Louis)
Joseph M. Daly Music Co, Boston
John R. Fuller, Temple, Texas
Carl Hoffman, Kansas City
Scott Joplin Music Co, St Louis; New York
   (also Scott Joplin, New York)
Victor Kremer, Chicago & New York
Leiter Bros, Syracuse
M. L. Mantell, Syracuse
A. W. Perry & Sons Music Co, Sedalia
Val A. Reis Music Co, St Louis
Will Rossiter, Chicago
Seminary Music Co, New York
S. Simon, St Louis
Robert Smith, Temple, Texas
Owen Spendthrift, St Louis
John Stark & Son, Sedalia, St Louis & New York
   (also Stark Music Co, St Louis & New York: Stark Music
      Printing & Publishing Co, St Louis & New York)
Joseph W. Stern, New York
Success Music Co, Chicago
Thiebes-Stierlin Music Co, St Louis
University Music Co, St Louis